Surviving In Stilettos

Inspiration to the Divas who are Young, Fabulous & dealing with the effects of Breast Cancer

DEETRIA N. CANNON

Published by Twenty-Two Publications

Copyright © 2014 by Deetria Cannon

All rights reserved.

No portion of this book may be reproduced or transmitted in any form or by any means, electronic or mechanical, including photocopying, recording, or by any information storage, without permission in writing from the author.

Deetria N. Cannon
Surviving In Stilettos

ISBN-10: 0692212701
Digital ISBN: 978-0692212707

Printed in the United States of America

www.survinginstilettos.com
www.wix.com/dnichole22/mystory

dnichole@legacy83.com

First Edition

Book design by Anthony Scott Jr. and Deetria Cannon

Interior Photograph: Devon Divine Hood
Back cover photo by: Mike O Images

~Surviving In Stilettos ~

DEDICATION

Thanks be to God for the inspiration and the ability.

To every person who has ever directly or indirectly been affected by breast cancer. Support the Fighters, Admire the Survivors, Honor the Taken.

To my beautiful Mother DeeEtta. You are God's gift to me, I am God's gift to you; and together two is better than one… I love you.

Ms. Adele Langham and Ms. Ashling Chantal, my pink ribbon sisters resting peacefully in heaven.

CONTENTS

Acknowledgement   i

   I. Why Me? Why Now? 4

   II. The Bold, Bald, & Beautiful .... .12

   III. Faith vs. Fear 17

   IV. Love Angels 28

   V. Pink Ribbon Sisterhood.......................36

   VI. Diagnosed & Dating..........................42

   VII. Emotional Rollercoaster 50

   VIII. Mirror Check 57

   IX. Pink Boas & Bone Aches 66

   X. Back on your Own 80

   XI. Live Out Loud 88

   XII. Praise & Purpose 91

   XIII. Facts of Life 95

~Surviving In Stilettos~

ACKNOWLEDGMENTS

I would like to acknowledge and give special thanks to my medical doctors and staff from Cadence Health and Central DuPage Hospital in Winfield, Illinois that take great care of my health providing excellence in every way.

Janet Jenkins from the Illinois Breast and Cervical Cancer Program; DuPage County Health Department. As well as *Shaneah Taylor*. You both went above and beyond your job descriptions as professionals making such an impact in my life.

To my family and close friends, I gratefully acknowledge your prayers, support, enthusiasm, and encouragement. Thank you for being there for me in so many ways showing your love start to finish during this sensitive time in my life. You know who you are.

Special thanks to my two *God Sisters* Dr. Muriel Jean-Jacques and Stephanie Jean-Jacques you are amazing in more ways than one. Every extra mile you went for me will always be appreciated and held close to my heart.

Special thanks to my dearest friend and *"Sista Girl"* Miya Brewer. Your spirit is one of a kind, and you gave me all you had to give during this time in my life. You are a special gem that will be treasured forever.

To my *"Auntie"* Mrs. Yvonne Calloway you were the voice to confirm that now was the time, and gave me the insight and fire to jumpstart my capabilities in Nov 2012, thank you, and *I did it!*

To the *Love of my life* Anthony Scott Jr. although you were not yet brought into my life during my journey, I am glad God answered my prayers after the storm sending me a God-fearing man who loves me for me unconditionally. Thank you for telling me I am beautiful every day, as well as being my support and partner on this amazing accomplishment. #DreamTeam

God bless you one and all, and thank you for loving me the way I love you. I hope you all are further inspired by this blessing from me to you.

PREFACE

There is a saying by an unknown author saying, *"If you don't have ups and downs, then that means you're not living."* If that isn't the truth! We are all born from our Mother's wombs, and once we are birthed into this great big world, the rest of our journey is controlled by God the creator of all things, including giving everything its own purpose. So many people go through life wondering what their purpose is; how they will figure it out, and how the heck will they make a difference once they find it! Until we find ourselves and our purpose, many of us feel our true destiny is not complete and we have just been coasting through this game called life. This book was inspired though my breast cancer diagnoses at the young age of twenty-six. I believe it is a part of my new found purpose to now share my story to and inspire those who have been directly or indirectly affected. Overtime this journey that consumed a year of my life as a patient, whipped me into shape mentally, physically, and built the strength I exude now emotionally. My purpose came to me one day as if cupid shot me with his arrow, and it was simply to be sensitive to the needs of others, while using my testimony to give hope, love, and laughter. I now strive to project encouragement into the lives of those God puts in my path.

As a breast cancer survivor since 2010 my story is one of perseverance, strength, and integrity growing as a woman and winning the fight against a silent killer to so many women and men when not detected early enough. Many people including myself at the time chose to keep this serious matter… a private matter. It took a long time for me to open up about it to anyone outside of my family circle. Since this type of diagnosis is rare for women under the age of forty to experience, there are very minimal resources or groups available for young women under the age of thirty to receive support from. Due to the lack of personal knowledge people have about cancer aside from the morbid assumption cancer equals death, it would have been really nice to have had someone close in age to relate to, and who understood my questions and concerns. Most women under the age of forty feel they are in a world of their own and have a hard time relating to the support groups that are available that are primarily women well over forty. So with that being said, this book is my gift to every young woman who is busy with life as a career woman, mom, wife, student, mogul, or just simply the hard work of being fabulous on a daily basis; and then getting a reality check in a moment's time that can interrupt your runway strut, knocking you out of your *Jimmy Choo's*!

When you go through a life changing event such as dealing with cancer, you cannot come out the same person. To this day I changed the way I eat, the way I live, the way I handle situations, and view the World now. Every morning when I open my eyes first thing I say is, *"Thank you Lord for waking me up this morning and granting me with the gift of this day."* Because someone somewhere else is fighting to survive. Hopefully, this information will be helpful to your pink ribbon journey whether you are a current or former patient, caretaker, or friend. The desire to take on the task of writing my own book as it relates to celebrating my *"survivorship"* has been long overdue. These chapters entail support, encouragement, and straight-no-chase information on how to deal with the effects of breast cancer as a young, fabulous, Diva trying to survive while rocking your stilettos!

1
Why Me! Why Now?

The term "Diva" has its pros and cons, however in this case we are embracing nothing except fabulous! A true Diva is one who behaves as a goddess or queen, and I am a strong believer that it does not mean arrogance. It is the way you carry yourself and show off your personality with confidence and individuality. Just because you aren't famous, doesn't mean you can't be a star or feel like one. Whether or not you are a successful business entrepreneur, doctor, celebrity, city socialite, stay-at-home Mom, teacher, model, student, athlete, or an author such as myself we all have two things in common our gender and our breasts; even if they are different cup sizes! No tax bracket, color of skin, educational degrees, or one's marital status can or will change that. We are busy living the lives in which God blessed us with, trying to fulfill each day making a difference in the lives of others personally or professionally while simply having fun!

When life is in motion, it is what we choose to make of it. We can either live out loud, or ride the day to day rollercoaster with a curve ball thrown in-between making sure we are awake and paying attention. You know those, *"Oh why me, why now?"* type curve balls from either your child's school calling in the middle of your day letting you know they got sick, an unwanted flat tire, having your car towed unexpectedly, a bad hair day, losing your favorite lipstick, having to work late, or even a petty argument with your significant other. But how is a Diva-on-the-go supposed to handle the ultimate unexpected? I am blessed to say that early detection saved my life, as many others when taken seriously. It was a cold December morning in 2009 when I found a small lump in my left breast similar to the size of a ping pong ball. As I performed a self-breast exam, like most I never really knew exactly what I looking for. That morning through my discovery and intuition, I knew something was wrong, because it didn't feel right. Now mind you, I learned all throughout my educational health classes the importance of self-exams and checking my own breasts, so that's why I kept it in the back of my mind. I often found myself doing a random check just in case, because I just thought I should. In my case I feel I was prompted by the Holy Spirit to do so. Your story may be the same or much different, but my first surgery which was a lumpectomy actually took place on one of my favorite casual holidays on April 1st, 2010 which was *"April Fool's Day."* Obviously the full day of events was no laughing matter, but I still managed to pull a good prank towards my nurse while waking up from being under heavy anesthesia. Hey! It's what I do! My story is unique because going into surgery they weren't expecting the mass to be cancerous, so there was supposed to be no pressure. After surgery my surgeon spoke with my Mom with an inquisitive look on her face explaining the details, and not quite sure what she saw attached to my chest wall. She assured she would be in touch soon with the pathology report. We can all fast forward to that one week later when the phone rings, and on the receiving end you get the news from your surgeon with a prognosis from recent test results being told, "*I am sorry, you have cancer.*" Regardless if you were told in person, over the phone, or even through a written letter, the reaction of "*WHAT!?*" still comes out the same. Who knows, it may have even been plus or minus some curse words! But believe it or not Diva, just like I did, you have to face this head-on starting now.

It's crazy how one conversation can change everything. As the room went cold, and life in that moment felt like it just stopped; I'm assuming your body went into an overdrive of emotions not knowing which one to express first. Sadness, Confusion, Fear, Anger, Denial, fought to be front and center. I know I remember getting light headed, and my eyes got big in disbelief, heart raced out of anxiety, and with little knowledge of what cancer was or what steps were next, fear seized the moment with the thought of, "*Am I going to die?*" Alone in my home in that moment, I hung up from the call with my surgeon, and called my Mom. As she answered the phone in her upbeat cheerful tone, I relayed the news crying over the phone like a newborn child. She was in disbelief yet still comforted me, and told me to come by the house. I was scared of what awaited, and wondered if I still had a future. I remember the rest of my day after I received that phone call like it was yesterday. I immediately felt lost, alone, and hopeless. It was April of 2010, and I put on an oversized fleece, and some baggy military pants not even caring if I matched or looked presentable to go run my errands. As I made a quick stop, I recall it being the first time I was in a public setting being around people even as complete strangers feeling like I had this huge plague of a secret. To walk past people in the aisles felt different, when no one knew my life changing news I was just told hours before. Some may wonder what would make that day different than any other time I would be amongst strangers carrying on with my day-to- day routine. My answer would be I felt different, and not in a good way. After I ran my small errands I went to my Mom's house, and although the sun was shining outside I was very sad and blue. I showed up at the front door, and my Mom looked at me like while chuckling to herself, *"What are you wearing?"* She knew I have always been the type to dress how I feel which is usually nothing less than fabulous, but the look she witnessed was screaming depression. She gave me encouraging words, prayer, and a Mother's protective embrace reassuring me all was going to be fine, but made sure I knew to not walk out the house looking a hot mess again. I'm too cute to be dressed crazy!

The unexpected had just intercepted my world in a flash of a second. The denial effect can be strong, not just for me but my family members also. Denial is one of the most common defense mechanisms that we all use, pretending that an uncomfortable thing did not happen. It also is one of the best-known defense mechanisms and it can work to protect the ego from anxiety. When you have a similar lifestyle profile of being young in your mid-twenties, no family history, hearing more conversation of a benign fibroadenoma verses a malignant cancerous tumor, living an active lifestyle, eating decently well, and avoided all harmful drugs, you can't help but to feel someone made a mistake possibly sleeping on their job when finalizing your pathology report. The moment of clarity arrives if you choose to receive a second opinion from another doctor. Once the same exact news is given to you then at that point you have to take in the confirmation, breathe deeply, and prepare yourself mentally, physically, and emotionally to start your journey.

So Diva, you are officially now diagnosed and probably wondering *what is next*, and how this whole medical world is going to fit and become a part of your already-so-busy life schedule, *right?* A serious illness as such can interrupt school, relationships, careers, wedding planning, and even the timing of having children. My calling after my journey is to empower young divas like you, reminding you when life gives you lemons, envision a lemon drop martini! Now that the news traveled fast within your family circle and everyone knows, now is the time to stand tall like RuPaul and be empowered by the lyrics of his song Supermodel, "*You Better Work!*" You have a life to live and people who need you on this Earth, so time for phase one which is listening and learning about your specific diagnosis, treatment options, getting a second opinion, scans, lab blood tests, arranging a caretaker if you have children, because this will consume about a year of your life. I am still able to recall when my breast surgeon told me the length of time this would take after our two hour meeting discussing the news with my family present. I didn't want to believe her. I thought for some reason, this cancer thing was short term, and I could maybe pop a prescription pill, run some tests, and I could be on my way… but boy was I wrong! The best advice I can give you for starters is to stay off the internet! Yes, I know we all love our Google and information access to the World Wide Web, however there is a thing I like to call *"information overload"* which I admittedly was guilty of creating for myself. You may find yourself spending hours on the computer or lying in bed scrolling on your phone on those sleepless nights going from breast cancer webpage to webpage, forums, medical journals, conspiracy theories, prospective cures, blogs, and the list goes on reading, wondering, jotting down notes, and even bookmarking things to show your doctor as though you're going to teach them something they perhaps missed in medical school. I don't think so! Overall, too much information can draw you too far in whereas it consumes you, and even though this is a new part of your life, it shouldn't become your life. Bedtime is a time to try and relax and let go of anxiety. Some deep breathing and a good-night blessing to you is a much better way drift off towards dreamland. Cancer is a diagnosis, not who you are. Aside from all of the basics, grab a hold of your faith, your prayer books, throw out all the junk food, load up on your immune vitamins, healthy meals, and keep your best friend on speed dial. Speak healing into your life, and believe in your heart that you are already healed by God and you will be a survivor, because you are surviving right now without even recognizing it! One way my Mother chose to take control away from this diagnosis was to refer to cancer as "*C*". To this day she strongly believes that words have power and when you speak it in the airways it gives it life to remain present having control. Since this wide spread disease of all forms has been taking over the lives of so many of our loved ones across the world, my Mother and I wanted to be two less people using the word and feeding into the power that has already achieved in the medical world, and I hope you and your team of support take part and make the change with us as time goes on.

If you feel the need, tell your friends and family to not claim you as being "*sick*" or even speak the "*C*" word around you. You may begin to feel a stress-free difference in the energy that is surrounding you. This is your life you're fighting for, and you are allowed to be in control of what your needs are at this time. The main rule of thumb your team of support needs to understand is to respect your wishes at all time making this an easy transition. All while keeping you in a positive mindset as much as possible, with your spirits high. The inspiration in sharing these moments with you is to be a reminder that once we accept the fact that our life experiences, the good and the bad, have purpose, we graduate to a higher level of understanding. Sometimes we have to remove ourselves emotionally from a situation so that we can see the lesson being revealed to us. As a young, fabulous diva like yourself, stop asking yourself *"why me?"* and start asking yourself *"why not me?" Why shouldn't I grow? Why shouldn't I grow closer to God? Why shouldn't I learn?* These are just some ways adversity helps us. Overall, you may not understand today or tomorrow, but eventually God will reveal why you went through everything you did.

Enjoy the little things, for one day you may look back and realize they were the big things. – Robert Brault

2
The Bold, Bald, & Beautiful

An American Psychiatric Association study reports that people who maintain an optimistic attitude may not only avoid depression, they may also improve their overall physical health. Our bodies respond to how we think and feel. This reaction is often referred to as the mind-body connection. The mind-body connection is the interplay between how our minds affect our bodies, and how our bodies affect our minds. Optimistic people seem to bounce back faster and prevent any stress related conditions from occurring. On the other hand people who are more pessimistic, who don't manage stress effectively, tend to get sick more often and have more physical complaints, experience more severe symptoms, and don't recover as well from illness. So my fellow Diva, keep that switch in your walk, your head held high, that shimmer in your smile, and life in your laugh because everything is going to be alright! God said so, and with that being said despite the current circumstances if you believe you are beautiful, everyone else will see it too.

Getting a cancer diagnosis is one thing, but to be told by your oncologist that chemotherapy is mandatory is a dreadful other that most young and fabulous divas such as yourself did not have on their "to-do" list. There are a few different treatment options depending on the type of cancer at hand, and some patients get to opt out of chemo and just do radiation which is to be on a prescription pill for the remainder of their lifespan. Although surely devastating news, you cannot let this diagnosis get you down. Instead, choose to embrace everything that this can possibly teach you. Most Divas have a big personality like Wendy Williams or can command the attention of any room like Mariah Carey. However, in situations like this many of us young women can experience a new shyness and experience new found insecurities having to deal with scars, physical changes, and now going bald. We know that life is short, and you have to now begin to open up and to allow yourself to form new friendships and bonds with fellow survivors or those extending their love and care that otherwise may have never came into your life. You have to trust that God has a way of getting your attention. He wants you to surrender control so you will put one hundred percent total trust in him.

Taking control of who you are, what you want to get out of this journey, and what will empower you in the process is all up to you. When it comes time to experience your hair transition due to the medication, you can either allow yourself to gradually go through the process and experience heavy shedding or baldness, or you can take control of your crown and glory and do it yourself alone or share the moment with a special friend. There is no right or wrong route to go. In June of 2010, I made a conscious decision for myself to take matters into my own hands. To be honest, it wasn't an easy decision; but it wasn't that hard. Those close to me knew I was always a big fan of wearing cute wigs of all kinds throughout the previous years anyways, due to enjoying change and being my own celebrity. Plus around this time model Amber Rose with her shaved head was a hot commodity, so I figured *why not?* I remember I went that hot sunny summer afternoon into a hair boutique near my home walking in with my request. To my surprise, the two male barbers that were there made an impact in my life that was so big I could never forget it even if I wanted too. As a first time customer the service was exceptional, but what mattered most was when I told them my story on why I needed to shave my hair off. The first barber assigned wasn't too comfortable with doing it, so the owner did it. They were both so supportive and encouraging showering me with compliments during and afterwards, that it actually turned an expected frown into a smile. I started out creating a moment by myself, but ended up sharing it with two new friends, and even got asked out on a date! I walked out of their hair boutique with an extra boost of confidence in my stilettos, all while feeling more beautiful than when I first entered. There was a new show-stopper in town, add me to the Hollywood A-list! Being bald and feeling beautiful while in treatment will have its challenges, but it doesn't have to slow you down. You will gain the confidence and begin to realize that others will need to accept you for who you are, which will be an overall very liberating experience. It will allow your true beauty, and God given facial features to stand out and shimmer. You deserve to look and feel great, while living a happy amazing life!

It is important to feel good about yourself during this transition. A big fear many of us go through when diagnosed, is not allowing people to treat us differently since we look different by having no hair. There are many websites and organizations that will help you find options to make you feel good while dealing with the hair loss if medically you can't avoid it. Baldness is typically a part of cancer for many women and should never be something we should have to be ashamed of or feel the need to hide. Although some Divas opt to make use of a new wig, I know everyone can't afford the cost and some may find them too uncomfortable. There are other beautiful options such as a jeweled headdress, cute hats, bandanas or scarves to work with your loss of hair. Realizing that we as young women affected by cancer already feel scared and vulnerable; it is important we still allow ourselves to look and feel feminine. It is during a process such as this; even more than any other time in your life that you need to feel as if you are still attractive. When you first lose your locks while facing cancer, many women are not mentally ready to face the world without something on their head. Trust me when I say that being bald is nothing to be ashamed of.

In the song lyrics by India Arie she sings, *"I am not my hair, I am not this skin, I am not your expectations. I am not my hair, I am not this skin, I am a soul that lives within."*

3
Faith vs. Fear

Faith and Fear have something in common. They both ask us to believe in something we cannot see. *Faith* tells us that no matter what lies ahead of us, God is already there. Breast cancer is treatable, although we all are still fighting for a cure. The traumatic fear associated with it is fully conquerable! Ladies, we can fight it and win! *"Though she be but little, she is fierce!"* — William Shakespeare said in *A Midsummer Night's Dream.* In most women's mind breast cancer is an automatic death sentence and an immediate fear that will rob one of any hope for life. According to Susan G. Komen for the Cure, while breast cancer is considered a *"woman's"* disease, 1 out every 100 cases of breast cancer occurs in men. At this moment I'm a four-year breast cancer survivor, going on forever by the grace of God. I am a fabulous daughter, sister, love of someone's life, and friend. I know all too well the suffocating fear associated with the mere thought of breast cancer. Almost as well as I know the pain of trying to squeeze into a shoe size too small just because they're on sale! Like you, I too lived it! I watched it grip my family as they struggled with the reality of my diagnosis. They all kept their faith and trusted in God's word. Although my faith is strong, I admit negative thoughts wondering if I would die would cross my mind. There were days when fear entered my imagination during those dark days on my journey, which made me wonder *would I ever get a chance to meet the love of my life and get married? Will I be in a position to ever have children down the road after going through chemotherapy? Will I be able to experience motherhood?* If you are currently a parent, I know there are times you fear your child or children growing up without you by their side. I feared having a lumpectomy and scars on my breasts and under my left arm from the sentinel lymph node dissection. I worried about what my future husband would think, because I no longer saw myself as *"normal"* moments when I would stand nude in the mirror while my war wounds stared back at me. On two separate occasions I had vivid dreams of Jesus Christ and God speaking to me giving me their peace. One was after a night of hysterically crying Jesus appeared in a dream showing me his face, and spoke calm words of comfort directly to me. Another dream included a powerful religious symbol, the burning bush which represents many things to Jews, Christians and Muslims such as God's miraculous energy, sacred light, illumination, and the burning heart of purity, love and clarity. From a human standpoint, it also represents Moses' reverence and fear before the divine presence. So to me I awoke with God's presence feeling secure that everything was going to be ok. God replaces your fear with faith, your pain with purpose, and your obstacles with opportunities. We cannot allow negative thoughts to live rent free in our mind. God wants you to live by faith not by sight. I was alive, still am, and so are you Diva! Most of my trust in God was not built or tested when everything was good. It was built when everything was crumbling before my eyes. Your journey will allow you to gain a deeper appreciation of the many paths available for connection to a higher power, spiritual fulfillment or to an increased sense of purpose and inner peace. The anxiety and pain I went through brought me to a spiritual rebirth of joy and brought me that peace through God as my rock. 2 Timothy 1:7 says, " For God has not given us the spirit of fear, but of power, of love, and of a sound mind." Being able to keep both breasts was a blessing, verses having to lose them to a double mastectomy opting for reconstruction like many tend to pursue to prevent reoccurrence. Although the reconstruction route still has its risks of leading to temporary self-image and self–esteem concerns, it enables women to now learn about implant and tissue flap procedures, as well as their nipple reconstruction options. A small percentage of women, including actress Angelina Jolie, "have genes that put them at a very high lifetime risk," a medical surgeon said. Media outlets explained that Jolie opted for a preventative double mastectomy after learning that she carried a mutation in a gene called BRCA1, which gave her an 87% chance of breast cancer. Although people expect us to remain so strong and in a positive frame of mind 24/7, I admit I was nervous about the three hours surgical procedure I agreed to have, as my first surgery ever. I hoped to function normally after it was over, and the size of my breast after the swelling would subside so I wouldn't look like I was a part of the circus! Thank God it all went well, miracles do exist! There is a funny story that my Dad and I still share to this day, that makes us laugh hysterically when we have flashbacks of this time in my life. After I came home following my second surgery which was a sentinel lymph node dissection in May 2010, I was at home resting in bed while my Dad was taking a nap in my living room. Well needless to say the pain medication from the hospital IV wore off and woke me up out of my sleep in massive pain. Since this was all so new to me not knowing what to expect, I panicked thinking something went terribly wrong with the drain my surgeon installed to catch the fluid from the incision under my left arm. Knowing that twenty-two of my God-given lymph nodes were outside of my body on a microscopic slide somewhere, I thought I did something wrong in my sleep to make the fluid back up in the tube causing my left breast puff up like a balloon. I woke up my Dad, and told him we need to go back to the hospital and to the ER! My Drama Queen was in full effect at this point, alert the press! We tried to tamper with it ourselves, only making matters worse, and let's just say we made a slight mess at the same time. Dad got me to the car on this preliminary summer day during Memorial Day weekend, but I probably would have been better off calling an ambulance. Through my tears and pain level between an 8-10, our car ride felt like it took forever! On this hectic day, I learned the importance of following the rules of the road to someone who works in transportation, because one violation can possibly put their job at risk. So let's just say, all while he is making complete stops and using his turn signal while changing lanes, I was trying not to lose my mind! Boy, what a wild and crazy day that was! Once the ER doctor checked everything out, I was given some new pain meds, and sent back home to rest. My Mom was calm upon our return like, *"I figured it was nothing to worry about."* Clearly, she knows her child!

Through it all I acknowledged my fears, but I never let them stop me. I coached myself to think and act in spite of my feelings. I pushed myself to read, ask questions, build a rapport with my doctors, and make necessary decisions for my overall well-being. Even to this day I still get a little nervous when getting my mammograms results and having to do blood work, but I eagerly do both because I know EARLY DETECTION SAVES LIVES! Every negative thought that crosses our minds from the enemy is a lie so keep believing! I also know that we possess the power and authority over all fear and negativity. For my spiritual warriors this is the time for you to rejoice always, pray without ceasing, In everything give thanks; For this is the will of God in Christ Jesus for you. 1 Thess 5:16-18 NKJV In the above verse, take note that it says "*in*" everything give thanks - it did not say "*for*" everything give thanks. In the midst of the trial, in the midst of the attack, when you feel as if the enemy is in your face with all of hell itself, right there, at that moment do not give in to the pressure of the devil. Instead turn the tables on him and put the pressure back on the devil where it belongs, lifting your hands to the Lord beginning to just love on God praising and worshiping Him. When we choose to transform our thoughts, change our perspectives, and alter our actions by having faith, fear loses control and power takes over. That's how I was able to fight my fears and get help. I knew immediately that I mattered more than the cancer, and that my faith in God would and had already begun my healing. I chose to focus on my desire to live, and living for the sake of my mother not only as her only child, but her best friend. Also for my fabulous future that awaited me, because the world wouldn't be the same without my shimmer, or yours Diva! So I faced the facts of my diagnosis and used the knowledge to become empowered in the fight for my life! Cancer or not, you can do the same and fight for yours, you have a lot to keep living for, you have people that not only love you, but NEED you! You have to believe that as long as you keep waking up in the morning, it's evidence that HE is not through with you.

Many people find any kind of uncertainty hard to live with, however the aim of cancer treatment for many people is to cure the cancer. In some cancers that are very slow-growing, or that have spread beyond their original area of the body, the aim may be to control the cancer and delay its progress. Many people choose not to work during their treatment. Going back to work after a break of a few weeks or months can be difficult, so you may feel that you're able to go back to your old job, but now feel nervous about it. Depending on the type of cancer and its position in the body, you may have symptoms such as tiredness, weight loss, breathlessness or pain. These may affect your ability to work. It may also be difficult to decide whether or not to work during your treatment, so it depends very much on your individual circumstances. It's natural to have a range of feelings and emotions when you have been diagnosed with cancer. Your emotions may make it difficult for you to concentrate or work effectively. You may need to take some time off to adjust to what is happening. Some people choose to carry on working, either full-time or part-time, during their treatment; while others need to carry on working as much as possible for financial reasons. I was in a position to take time off for six months, since I worked as a recruiting consultant for a large oil and gas company at the time. The only person I disclosed my medical concerns with was my manager due to her being a former family friend. Otherwise I preferred the workplace to not know my business. Talking about my diagnosis was very difficult and still can be to this moment… even four years later. I don't know about you, but I could barely keep my composure without bursting into tears having to hear myself say out loud to someone that, "*I have breast cancer.*" So you may worry about how your colleagues will react, or whether they might withdraw from you. You may worry that talking about your current health status might make things awkward for yourself or your colleagues in the workplace. Some people may avoid you because they don't know what to say and are afraid of saying the wrong thing. You can help them by bringing up the subject and showing that you're willing to talk about it. Informing your colleagues can help more than hurt, because they'll know what to expect. For example, if fatigue affects your moods or concentration, it gives them the opportunity to support you. If you don't want to tell colleagues then *Hunnie* that's your *"prerogative,"* like Bobby Brown said! For some people it's the right thing not to tell colleagues that they have cancer, because it's fair for you to try and keep one area of your life as normal as possible. This is a good way of coping for some people. There is no right or wrong way to handle your life during your diagnosis, you are in control and have to do what works bests for you. Confidence doesn't come when you have all the answers; it comes when you are ready to face all the questions.

We all have economic realities in our lives, and medical emergencies can cause financial stress. In the acute phases, there may be lost income owing to missed work time or a smaller disability check. There likely have been additional expenses related to non-covered medical bills, childcare, transportation, or more take-out food. There is the well-known phenomenon every diva has experienced called *"retail therapy"* that can result in large unwanted credit card bills. There may also be long-term financial implications. Thanks to the Americans With Disabilities Act, it is illegal to discriminate against someone at work because of cancer or another disability. Research has shown that most employers do not discriminate against employees who are diagnosed with cancer and are having treatment. Your employer should provide help and support to enable you to do your job. The practical reality, however, is that it is almost impossible to prove that a missed promotion or denied new position could be due to your medical history. There are many myths and misunderstandings about cancer. As silly as it sounds, some of your colleagues may worry that they can catch cancer, but cancer can't be passed on like an infection and the people you work with have no risk of catching it. Some people may also worry that they could be harmed if you're having treatments such as chemotherapy or radiotherapy, again there's no risk to your colleagues, family, or friends. Chemotherapy is broken down in the body and can't harm anyone you come into contact with; and radiotherapy treatment from an external machine doesn't make you radioactive.

Dealing with the effects of your diagnosis will allow you to examine your life and to think carefully about priorities and time. Working during your treatment gives you satisfaction and helps you to focus on something other than what's going on with your health. It also may cause you to feel that time may be more limited, making you push even harder to achieve goals. Depending on the type of work you do, and whether you have anyone else who can help out for a while, can be the deciding factor to realize your work life is less important and to go ahead and reduce your professional responsibilities at this time. That decision can also be made based on your health, the type of cancer you have, and what kind of treatment you choose. It's impossible to say how you will react to treatment until you start. This uncertainty makes it hard to look ahead and decide how much work to take on. It will help to let your employer know this upfront so that they are aware you may need to change your work plans at short notice. The central truth is that a diagnosis of cancer will impact your professional life as a woman, and it is helpful to acknowledge this, reminding yourself that there are lawyers, career consultants, financial planners, and others who can be helpful, if necessary so you won't feel like stepping away will cause things to fall out of order. There are ways to allow priority for your health needs while you keep working, let your faith give you the strength to make the best decisions for you.

When you're thinking about working while having treatment, ask yourself some questions:

- *Can I cut back on my workload temporarily?*

- *Can I work in a different way to allow time for rest as well as my treatments?*

- *Who can help me in practical ways?*

- *Where can I get extra financial help to get me and my family through this period?*

- *Is it safe for me and for others if I carry on working during treatment?*

"Focus on the powerful, euphoric, magical, synchronistic, beautiful parts of life, and the universe will keep giving them to you."

- *Unknown*

4
Love Angels

A love angel is someone who brings encouragement, love, hope, peace, and comfort to a person during difficult circumstances. Whether grieving the loss of a family member or suffering from a serious illness, disability, or tragedy. Before your diagnosis you were busy with life doing your own thing at your own time, being a productive citizen of society, and sometimes one of the hardest people to catch up to I can assume. In the words of Kelly Clarkson many of us strong women can be described as, *"Miss Independent, Miss Self-sufficient, Miss Keep-your-distance, Miss Unafraid, Miss Outta-my-way, Miss Don't-let-a-man-interfere, Miss On-her-own, Miss Almost-grown,"* at some point in our lives. What needs to be realized is the fact that it is simply okay to ask for help and to let go of the control, and hang up the Superwoman cape for a while. Support can come from many different sources, accept the opportunities to lean on your friends, family, coworkers, spouse/partner, and/or volunteers that want to help you with cooking, cleaning, errands, childcare etc. and give you time to rest and take a moment for yourself to recoup in between your treatments and doctor visits. Your friends may still not fully understand the anxiety you're going through, but they will likely be more appreciative of the struggle and admire you for it. Ask yourself, *what kind of help do I really need now and in the near future?* It's one thing to live life with a diva mentality, but now is your chance to be pampered and spoiled while you heal mentally and physically, you won't regret it I promise! The family and friends you choose to include in this personal part of your life become your inner circle of support during cancer treatment and will be needed to help you get through this. My Mom's close friend who I call "*Aunt*" Thea came by one day while I was at home resting, and brought me a hearty yet still healthy Thanksgiving type dinner on a regular weekday just to see me smile. That meal definitely gave me life! It not only made me feel good to know she gave me her time, but I'm sure it made her feel even better knowing on the inside that her good deed was valued and appreciated. I received a number of lovely flower deliveries every few weeks, which anyone that knows me knows I absolutely love flowers! I had close friends and family stop by my house, or my Moms house to spend a little time with me or get me outside when time allowed, which always lifted my spirits. Another example of amazing love angels stems from when my Mom arranged not one but two surprise birthday parties for me in August 2010. She has always been the woman to go above and beyond for me, not just because I am her only child, but simply because of the way her heart beats for the ones she loves. One of my best of friends from high school Miya, and my Aunt Thea also helped with the planning. My pink nail spa party with my closest family and friends was such a great time. We had a private room to get our pedicures, share laughs, eat cake, food, and of course open presents! Even though most divas love a great gift, the gifts that mattered most that day was my breath of life to celebrate another birthday, and the love and support I received from those in attendance. The nail spa even donated a portion of the proceeds to Susan G. Komen in my name. Overall, it was heart-warming and such a thoughtful blessing. I had a slight notion about the second surprise party, so I made sure I dressed cute and threw on my stilettos just in case for this one! I was correct, and the venue that hosted my party was a local upscale movie theatre where my Mom arranged a photo slideshow of my life, which included heartfelt messages written from my family and friends far and near to be shown on the BIG screen! Talk about the wow factor, and watching a tear jerker! One of my girlfriends from out of state arranged for a gorgeous pink ribbon zebra print custom cake to be designed in my honor that screamed *fabulosity*! Many were in attendance, and enjoyed the day seeing me smile and knowing that I was recovering to good health while staying strong beautifully inside and out. Those memories of love and care will last a lifetime. I was officially twenty-seven.

Medical expertise is a key part of your cancer treatment, but it won't be enough. Having good support at home and around you is crucial. "A cancer diagnosis adds an enormous amount of stress to a person's life," says Harold J. Burstein, MD, a staff oncologist at the Dana-Farber

Cancer Institute in Boston. "But people who have strong social supports -- good friends and family -- tend to cope much better." The following gives insight on ways to allow people to support you, putting life a little bit more at ease during this time. However, keep in mind some of these same principles can be applied towards the caretaker. People fail to realize that sometimes the primary support needs support also.

Don't be afraid to ask for help. You may feel awkward about asking friends or family for help. You may not want to impose. But you need help right now Diva. You can't get through treatment by yourself. So summons up your courage and ask. You may be surprised at how willing people are to pitch in. In fact, they may just be waiting for you to ask. *"Courage is one step ahead of fear." – Coleman Young*

- **Build a team.** Don't lean too much on one person. Instead, ask for help from several people. That way, you won't feel guilty about imposing too much on one person, and no relative or friend will feel overwhelmed. When asking for cancer support, play to the strengths of individual friends and family, says Terri Ades, MS, APRN-BC, AOCN, director of cancer information at the American Cancer Society in Atlanta. Ask a methodical, organized friend to help you come up with a schedule and work out the logistics of planning treatments. Ask your family member or friend "the chef" to prepare dinners that you can freeze and reheat as needed. Obviously, your closest family members such as your spouse, children, or parents are likely to be at your side through this. But they may not always be the most helpful cancer supports, says Ades. They're going to be frightened and upset just like you. So for some types of support, friends who are a little further removed may be more helpful by surprise.

- **Bring a partner to appointments.** Obviously, a friend or family member can offer emotional support during doctor's appointments or treatments. But he or she can also have an important practical role in cancer support. During the appointment, a partner might remember details or questions that you forget. "It's great to have a second set of ears in these meetings," says Jan C. Buckner, MD, chair of medical oncology at the Mayo Clinic in Rochester, Minn.

- **Figure out what you need and ask for it.** A lot of people may want to help but aren't sure what to do. If you don't give them guidance, they may do things that you don't really want. So figure out what sort of cancer support you need. Do you want someone to watch the kids while you take a nap? Do you need someone to drive you to chemotherapy? Or do you just want a pal who will go to dinner and the movies -- without saying a word about your cancer? Decide what you need and then ask for it.

- **Talk to your children.** Parents want to protect their children, and many don't want to tell their kids about a cancer diagnosis. However, that's the worst thing you could do. Your kids are going to find out whether you tell them or not, so it's better to talk to them now so you can control how they learn about it. Obviously, you need to adjust the information depending on the age of your child: a teenager will require a lot more detail than a 4-year-old. But all children will be worried; not only about you, but also about how their own lives will change. Be sure to reassure them that their needs won't be neglected and someone will always take care of them. Children generally resume their normal routines and their natural styles long before the end of treatment. Taking care of yourself during your treatment is an important part of the healing process. This includes your physical, mental, emotional and spiritual well-being.

Research according to Breastfriends.com informs the following:

Nourishing your Body

- Limit liquids with your meals. It allows your digestive juices to work at full strength which will reduce indigestion

- Drink plenty of liquids between meals to stay hydrated.

- Eat smaller, more frequent meals; it will reduce the stress on your digestive system.

- Eat plenty of fruit, fresh is best. Eat lots of fresh vegetables, either steamed or boiled.

- Include fruit and vegetable juices in your diet.

- Avoid fatty foods and sugary foods.

- Take vitamin & fiber supplements to help build back the immune system.

- Keep your muscles limber by doing some basic stretches.

- Get plenty of exercise, fresh air, relaxation and fun.

- Ginger & peppermint tea can settle your stomach.

- Eat a whole foods diet with grains and low fat protein sources.

- Avoid alcohol, tobacco, dairy products, red meats, fried, processed and fast foods.

Be careful not to do too much in the beginning. You may or may not have drain tubes in your chest depending on the type of surgery. It can be a week or two before they are removed. You will want to avoid all physical activity until they are removed. Check with your doctor.

Start to exercise as soon as possible, but take it easy. Go for a walk and look at the flowers. Just get moving and it will help your attitude as well as your health. If you like to garden, stroll around the neighborhood and see how others are using color in their yards. Be careful of the sun, chemo can sometimes make your skin even more sensitive. Wear a hat and sunscreen out in the sun. Try to take walks or swim in the early morning or after sunset. Check with your doctors first though to make sure that it is okay to exercise.

I believe that no woman should go through the cancer experience alone, and we know that often even the closest of our friends and family are at a loss to really know how to help. People's participation in maintaining your emotional, mental, physical and spiritual well-being is the foundation for the success of your full recovery. There is a profound author by the name of Dr. Gary Chapman, who wrote the book "The 5 Love Languages". Although the principles are geared towards relationships and marriage, I like to apply them towards my personal relationships which include my family and friends. The principles fall under these five categories: Quality Time, Gifts of Love, Acts of Service, Physical Touch, and Words of Affirmation. All five of these actions are what the *love angels* in your life should be exemplifying at this time. I saved every motivational get well card I received, as well as birthday cards with well wishes and prayers. If I had to count them all I probably have over one hundred. I have special pink ribbon bracelets I still wear to this day on occasion that were given to me from my Mom, my sister Keva, sister Krystina, and even a neighbor at the time Kimberly. Each gift of love and act of service carries a unique and special meaning to my heart I could never forget. The moral of this story is that no cancer patient should ever feel alone. To finish the remaining song lyrics of Kelly Clarkson, *"By keeping her heart protected, she'd never ever feel rejected. Little Miss Apprehensive…What happened to Miss Independent? No longer need to be defensive. Goodbye, old you, when love is true."*

5
Pink Ribbon Sisterhood

The politically correct definition of a sister is defined as a female who has one or both parents in common with another. However, many of us have learned in life that good friends are the family we choose. A sisterhood is defined as a state or relationship of being a sister or sisters… the quality of being sisterly. Going through breast cancer is one thing, but being blessed to help other women in the process or as a healthy survivor is another. We as women must believe in other women. We must uplift women, empower women, support women whenever and however we can in this pink ribbon sisterhood. No matter the individual differences we all will share a pink ribbon story of our journey that not everyone will be able to understand or relate too, but we can. We are all special; we are strong, and fabulous!

Now, by there being a multitude of different ways each woman has to deal with her procedures or treatments it all ends up taking a toll on us mentally. Remember that you should never be ashamed of your scars, because it's a reminder that you were stronger than whatever tried to hurt you. Being a part of the pink sisterhood we know that going through a lumpectomy, mastectomy, or double mastectomy is the worst part of dealing with the effects of breast cancer. It gives a state of shock and sense of loss. It also initiates a devastated state of mind to have to cope with and adjust within one's sexual identity worrying about how your partner may react, which is quite normal. Worst case scenario that can come from this would be acute grief that may last several months to a year before your feeling like yourself again and in good spirits regaining your confidence, however time heals all.

At this time in your life learn to embrace your family and friends. They all won't know the right words to say and how to comfort you, but at least give them the chance to try. Think positively by looking at your glass half full verses half empty at this point in time, it really does help. You are alive and your physician may be able to provide you with reconstruction options to give you a natural look and feel. Although you may not be accustomed to doing so, be open to accepting help from others, because you are taking on so much medically. Friends and family members will want to help but won't necessarily know what to do, so help them help you. Diva, enjoy this time off to heal and recuperate. Going through so many emotional and physical changes from your skin, hair, nails, eyelashes, and even losing your eyebrows can take a toll on you, but the one thing that can never change is your smile. It's the most beautiful asset on a woman....on you! Here are some ideas that can help you out:

- Create a list of chores, errands and tasks that you can have on hand when people ask what they can do for you and your family.
- Take photos to remember this journey.
- Have friends capture those moments where you shaved your head, or sat in the chemo room, or joked around with others you love.
- Model your favorite the hats and scarves for the camera. Put all these shots in a special book so you can remember and celebrate often.
- If you like to scrapbook or post on social media select some fun photos of family and friends that will make you smile and remember good times.

In this sisterhood, you will meet many people with unique stories and similar scars. Your major surgery comes with many coping options, and giving therapy a chance is one of them. Sadness, depressed moods, anxiety, and fear are all normal responses to a mastectomy, but if you find yourself having more bad days than good, or if your sleep patterns are being disrupted, you should seek help. Feel comfortable talking to your physician or oncologist about it so they can provide a referral. From one pink sister to another, the best advice I can give is to do what you love to bring your joy back in your life. When one door closes, another one is sure to open. Two months after my lumpectomy and sentinel lymph node dissection I was able to dance and choreograph again using a full range of mobility on my left upper side, something I feared I wouldn't be able to do as well any longer. God specializes in the impossible!

Some people have an easier time sharing feelings than others. It is okay if you feel more comfortable just listening. *Why do you need support you are probably wondering?* Because, my beautiful Diva no one should face this battle alone. When it comes to support groups some people find both individual and group sessions helpful. Belonging to a group where you can discuss anything and everything is very freeing. There are different kinds of support groups led by professionals such as psychologists, psychiatrists, oncology social workers, oncology nurses, or even local pastors. Other groups are led by breast cancer survivors. You can talk about everything from medical treatments to lack of sexual interest, to emotional rollercoaster's you may be dealing with. According to the Susan G. Komen website (ww5.komen.org) There are three main types of support: informational, emotional and practical. You may need different kinds of support at different times during your treatment and recovery. Also, you may want or need different kinds of support from different people. Social support may reduce: Anxiety and stress, emotional distress and depression, fatigue, the experience of pain. Social support may improve: Mood, self-image, the ability to cope with stress, sexual function and enjoyment, feelings of control. Pain is a part of life; it is what makes us human; it shapes us the same as love and laughter. You don't have to forget, but you cannot let it destroy you. Conquer the pain, don't let it conquer you.

The loneliness and isolation that so many feel when they are going through the breast cancer journey can be helped, if not erased, with the support, love, and care of total strangers that become new friends. I admit I tried my best to avoid support groups and one-on-one therapy when I was going through my struggle. The feeling of being venerable and opening up emotionally to a group of people or a "shrink" was just something I preferred to avoid until I was finally ready and realized it could help more than hinder me. You may find yourself trying to hide behind your smile as I did, while giving the appearance that everything is just fine when it's not. Or as though you are strong, yet you really are starting to feel weak. You have to find your release someway somehow, and get it out of you to feel better and emotionally free. Don't go in with the mindset of you not wanting to hear strangers' problems. Recognize that sharing induces the healing process and can create lifetime friendships. A foundation in my local area called, *Wellness House* helped me in many good ways. I took advantage of some of the programs they offered that I felt could help me relax or bond with someone who understands. *Wellness House* isn't a hospital or a clinic; they are literally a warm, welcoming gorgeous home/business filled with people, and programs, that are there to help.

They assisted in my healing process, and to regain my strength. Online groups such as Imerman Angels and Young Survival Coalition (www.imermanangels.org *and* www.youngsurvival.org) are starting possibilities for those not ready to reach out in person, but will have the chance to connect with and lean on someone who has went through the same battle with the same diagnosis. Although tears are bound to fall in any support group while opening up and expressing your thoughts, experiences, and feelings, don't assume it is solely a crying session; there is actually a lot of humor and inspiration that can be fulfilling. Use your voice for kindness, your ears for compassion, your hands for charity, your mind for truth, and your Heart for Love.

6

Diagnosed & Dating

Diva, you are your inspiration, you are your solution, you are your motivation. You may currently be young, single and still have your whole life ahead of you so don't let this setback stop your show! Every setback is a setup for a comeback. God wants to bring you out better than before. So before getting involved in dating you have to love yourself first. Sex and love should not be off the table now because this ugly diagnosis intercepted your life plans. Granted, there is a time and a place for everything, but sometimes you just meet someone or want to continue to look for someone special if that was something you were interested in before you got diagnosed. Biblically Proverbs 31:10 says, *"Who can find a virtuous woman? For her price is far above rubies."* You have to trust your struggle and realize once the dust settles, you are a priceless gem…you are a survivor. Strong is the new beautiful and it has nothing to do with looks. It's how you are as a person and how you make others feel. I know you are in the process of accepting your new body image that may be challenging for you to feel comfortable with, but it's not the end of the world. You are more than what you see. I have always been pretty comfortable with myself (inside and out). That is not to say that I am exceptional; I just have always been very self-accepting. I still feel that way. I adapted to my new body image with a fair amount of ease. The thought of dating during or after your diagnosis and treatment might make you nervous, exhilarated, cautious or curious. The physical and emotional changes you have faced including surgery, reconstruction, lymphedema, hair loss, skin changes, weight gain and infertility can leave you wondering; *Will prospective dates find me attractive? How do I tell someone about my diagnosis? What do I do if I lack energy or lose interest in sex?* These are very valuable concerns, but don't disconnect yourself from the dating game, before you even get started. Walking, dancing and even a self-massage help improve your body image and reduce stress/anxiety. Through confident posture and calm deep breathing you can reclaim your good feelings when your thoughts become critical of your body. Be sure to constantly remind yourself of your strength and resilience, it will exude your confidence from within.

"You are imperfect. Permanently and inevitably flawed. And you are beautiful." – Amy Bloom

Single women face special challenges during and after breast cancer. It is never easy dating and certainly a serious medical history does not make it easier. Diva, you can be reassured of one solid truth: that any partner worth having will not be scared away by your past or present illness. Take small steps; recognize that the uncertainty of dating always takes courage to take the risk to meet, know, and love someone. Now it may take even more. Your prospective partner may have worries about sharing experiences with you too; everyone typically has some sort of health history. A good way to ease into the dating scene is in low- pressure social settings, like a trusted friend's social gathering, or even an upscale chic lounge. You could join a group focused on activities that you enjoy, where you may find people with similar interests. For many fabulous divas dealing with the effects of breast cancer, the greatest worry is how a date or partner will react to hearing about your experience with breast cancer and seeing any physical changes caused by treatment. Your diagnosis may bring challenges in love, sex, and intimacy, but a crisis has a way of drawing a couple closer or even a potential couple starting off as friends. For those looking to date while diagnosed, here are a few do's and don'ts that may help:

- ***Do recognize that each situation will differ, depending on whom you're dating and how you feel.***

- ***Do look for someone that could be a friend first***

- ***Do feel free to wait a few dates to see the content of their character and if they are even worth knowing your personal business to that magnitude. Trust your judgment.***

- *Do choose a neutral place and a relaxed time to talk, where you both feel at ease.*

- *Don't feel rushed into telling everything about your life right away, including your diagnosis.*

- *Don't make excuses or feel less than if your date can't handle the fact that you've had breast cancer.*

- *Don't waste energy trying to change the situation if a guy is a loser and unsupportive. God has better awaiting you.*

- *Don't rush into being physical; let a man get to know you-for-you accepting your spirit not just your sexuality.*

Life, love, and relationships are to be lived in the moment. Living in the moment is all about living like there is no tomorrow. You must realize the beauty in every moment, as well in simple everyday activities or events that you may be a part of. Start dancing like nobody's watching! Time to be more optimistic, who cares what people may say, do, or think…it's your life, so it's your rules! If you want to have a reason to doll up, throw on your favorite pair of stilettos, primp and pamper yourself, and apply your favorite MAC lip gloss while walking out the door to go on a hot date, then Diva who is anyone to stop you? Tomorrow isn't promised, and with everything you are dealing with on a day-to-day basis it's important to do things that are going to take your mind off of it all; while allowing yourself to enjoy each moment created.

I was single and still in a position to mingle despite being in chemotherapy treatment for five months on a bi-weekly basis, and then a low side-effect weekly taxol steroid treatment for my last 3 months until December 2010. Even though some weeks would be better than others emotionally and mentally, when I was having a good day I tried my best to embrace it! I would focus on the importance of maintaining normalcy in my life, not playing the "*ill*" card forcing myself to feel alone, when I didn't have to be alone. You don't have to hide in your house or sleep the day away out of depression. My Mom was a big help in that aspect, she would plan local outings for us having us go shopping or spend a day at the movies. I would doll up and still go to a weekend club on occasion to dance with my friends for a change of scenery. I chose for preventive maintenance to become a non-drinker that whole year from the day I was diagnosed. I cut out everything I thought could set me back, instead of progress me forward, even any extra sugars. When your life is on the line, it's easier to say *no* to peer pressure in social settings, because you've adapted to a new experience. My personal past time as a hopeless romantic at that time still looking for love, would consist of browsing the online personals of a very popular dating site. My heart, cute face, smile, style, and great physique hadn't changed; so despite what my body was going through, I still deserved to enjoy a good time in good company. I was the type to always take a chance, because I never knew how absolutely perfect something *could* turn out to be. When I informed people that I didn't drink alcohol it was funny to the get reactions or hear responses from off the other side of the fence. By surprise, they were all more positive than I assumed them to be. People seemed to look at me as choosing the high road making better health conscious choices than the vast majority. I wasn't looking to be praised for my decision, because only I knew the motive behind that lifestyle choice. I recall getting to know this one guy briefly during my treatments and he casually offered me some Oreo cookies, which were once a favorite of mine. I hadn't opened up to him about what was really going on in my life, and at this time I was so strict about my health and my intake of things that could hurt me versus help me. I was cautious about everything I consumed during this time in my life, which also included refined sugars. So to not seem strange, I literally pretended to chew the Oreo's, when I actually crumbled them up in my pocket. There was another occasion when the same guy took me to see a play, and there was a scene that related to the death of one's Mother due to breast cancer. As hard as it was I kept my composure and emotions quietly to myself, having to be discreet about the tears and fear I felt. I wasn't just watching a moment on stage, I was stuck in that moment wondering about myself. Overall, my self-will made the transition easier than expected. I didn't want to just live; I wanted to continue to feel alive!

Now depending on whether your current relationship status is single, in a relationship, or married when it comes to sexual relations it can either be a priority or not even on the to-do list at this point during your life. This diagnosis honestly can either make or break a relationship or even a marriage due to all the components and unexpected hurdles that can be hard to overcome. Husbands and partners are relieved when your treatment is finally done and may likely be exhausted by the extra roles they have assumed. They worry about you as their wife or love of their life. The thought of possible death and how they would manage alone is where their strength may break down. Your man will try and protect you during this time and not express these fears. You may be interpreting this silence as indifference or misunderstanding, but don't. Many couples need time and, sometimes, help to find their way back to one another and to find the separate but parallel paths that continue together on the journey of life.

Be aware that your body is going to go through a lot of different changes like hot flashes due to pre-menopause during chemo and occasional vaginal dryness. I never noticed the change in that way, because realistically I was not active due to my own health precautions knowing my body being at risk to more due to a fluctuating white blood cell count. *So less was more to me at this time, okay*! Take time to talk to your guy about it, he needs to understand how you feel and that your sex drive will return sooner than later, and may even come back with a vengeance! Make it a priority to accept your new body - gradually get used to the way you look naked now. Stand in front of the mirror and identify three positive things about your body. If you have trouble with your partner seeing you naked, especially when having sex, wear lingerie or something that makes you feel good about yourself. Light the room with candles when you go to bed, even if the two of you are just going to have pillow talk. Most women are fortunate enough to say this whole experience made their union with their partner stronger. Let your partner, husband, or boyfriend climb in the trenches with you. Let them help in any way he wants. Give your mate permission to be as involved as he wants, keep him informed, and remember that not every man can climb in the trench with you so be grateful and show your appreciation. Remember, on days you're not feeling well, don't concern yourself with anything except feeling better. *Life is a onetime offer, use it well!*

7

Emotional Rollercoaster

I've had my share of ups and downs, but one thing I know the Lord has been good to me. Diva, you have to choose your thoughts carefully, keep what brings you peace, release what brings you suffering, and know that happiness is a thought away. Everyone wants happiness, no one wants pain; but you can't make a rainbow, without a little rain *right?* The truth is, finding out you have breast cancer is that grey cloud that you never wanted to drift your direction. There are so many emotions to sort through at this time: anger, guilt, sadness, fear, resentment, to name a few. Every inspirational-super strong- breast cancer survivor- turned advocate started out miserable, guaranteed. When people are first diagnosed with cancer and go into treatment, they enter an "adjustment period, coming face-to-face with the losses associated with cancer," says Karen R. Monaghan, LICSW, a clinical oncology social worker at Dana-Farber Cancer Institute in Boston. "They're very afraid—of going into surgery and what happens. Afraid of the pain and what they'll look like. *'Am I going to survive this?' 'Am I going to feel attractive ever again?'* They're pissed off that they're going to lose their hair, then they beat themselves up—*'I'm being vain and shallow.'*" Most of us, can't fathom experiencing so many emotions at one time, but the fact that there is no going back to *"before"* is what ends up being the hardest part to grasp. Emotions are a powerful force, so in order to find long-lasting achievement in life; you need to understand how to take control of them.

Diva, be aware that you may find yourself struggling with your diagnosis and suddenly on an emotional roller coaster. Sometimes you may feel shut down and numb, some days you may feel like Xena the Warrior Princess, and then there are times when you may feel flooded with myriad feelings, many of them intense and confusing causing you to just breakdown screaming and crying. I've been through all the above myself on many occasions, so you are not alone. An understanding of the critical inner voice and the impact it has on the emotional state of yourself at this time is a valuable psychological tool for you since you may still be grappling with your reactions to your *"new normal."* As Dr. Dean Ornish advises, "Stress promotes cancer growth; it suppresses your own immune surveillance system. Stress comes not so much from what we do but more importantly from how we react to what we do." When negative emotions such as anger and hatred are held on to, they actually suppress the immune system and promote cancer. Because negative emotions are promoted by the critical inner voice, it is important to deal with your voice attacks as part of dealing with your emotions.
In Breast Cancer: The Path of Wellness & Healing, Kathy Freston recommends asking, "*What is the anger in me that*

needs to be looked at? Is there some old wound that I need to tend to? Am I leaving this section of my life in a clean way so that I can start the next chapter of my life fresh, clean, healed without any of that old dark energy pulling me down?" Moral of this story is let people love you. A friend who understands your tears is much more valuable than a lot of friends who only know your smile. Be gentle with yourself, you're doing the best you can.

You will not always feel the way you do now. Some days are sure to be better than others. When it comes to the physical toll from your medications, experiencing the fatigue and achiness in your body during treatment and for a longtime afterwards it can make you wonder *"Will I always feel this way?"* Sometimes chemotherapy causes long term side effects. You will probably feel tired for some time after your treatment has finished. For some people, it can take up to a year to get their energy back. Cognitive changes after chemotherapy have recently been documented and have proven that *"chemo brain"* does exist! A UCLA study has shown that chemotherapy can change the blood flow and metabolism of the brain in ways that can linger for 10 years or more after treatment. One funny situation about a seven months after I finished my radiation treatment and was completely on my recovery as a survivor, I experienced what I think an episode of *"chemo brain"* while enjoying the fourth of July holiday with my step-sister and friend. Somehow I forgot where I parked, and was under the impression I got towed in the City of Chicago, when the officer could not find a trace of my car in any impound, they came to the conclusion it must have been stolen. I lost it completely, and called my Mom crying twenty-five miles from home in disbelief that this would happen to me. After using about an hour and a half of our time and all my emotions, we go back to the location with the officers who took the report, and my friend at the time chooses to walk down the same sidewalk a little further from where we were parked jus to double check, to come back telling me she had good news. While sobbing and wiping my tears I said, *"What?"* she said, *"I found your car!"* ... long story short, I was super embarrassed as though I had just been pranked on a hidden camera show, and so relieved and grateful at the same time. I thanked the officers and apologized for consuming their time, called my mom back with the news, and was so glad my girl followed her instinct to check the same location twice. Talk about a foggy brain!

When you are flying in a plane for example, there is always a chance of something happening, or even when you drive in a car to and from work. But, you can't let your mind play those games with you worrying about the *"what ifs."* You must control your mind. When I fly, I don't think of the plane falling, or turbulence that may occur disrupting my rest. If it happens I have no control over it, the pilots do. I can't just go into a fit because that will make matters worse, and I can't lose myself by being scared or worried, because I know I won't gain anything by doing that. I get on a plane knowing that I will not have any control while up in the clouds but the pilots will, as well as having security in my faith in God for a safe departure/arrival to my destination. It's the same with your diagnosis. You don't have control over the tumor(s), but the doctors and medicine do. You have control over your mind and emotions, and it's up to you to not let them go. Don't worry yourself sick, because all it will do will get you sick. And although some may consider you already "*sick*", you don't have to feel "*sick*" because you don't have to allow yourself to feel "*sick*"…*get it*?! Stay in control girlfriend! Alternative therapies to relax or de-stress include, a massage, acupuncture, Reiki, qigong, or meditation. Some patients also find these techniques helpful in combating some of the side effects of their chemotherapy.

When life gives you every reason to be negative, think of all the reasons to be positive. There is always someone who has it worse. Most people who live through their diagnosis, treatment and recovery will express sadness, fear, anger and confusion, along with many other forms of emotions during and even post-treatment. Depression is more than just feeling down in the dumps or sad for a few days. Feelings of depression don't go away and can interfere with your everyday life if you let it. I recently, read through my pink journal diary that was given to me by my Mother to host all my thoughts and feelings through my journey, and man it made me cry all over again. I didn't realize how much in the struggle I was at the time, compared to how full of life I am now. It feels good to feel great again, and sharing my shimmer of positivity; that is until PMS arrives like a demonic spawn ha! My writings at times during my journey were dark, and I had the clear signs and expressions that signaled depression. The thing that was difficult to accept and face in that moment, I had no clue I was actually feeling that way or even understood the magnitude of my emotions I was unveiling, because I hid behind my smile. These feelings are complex conditions, resulting from and affected by many factors: your diagnosis and treatment, aging, hormonal changes, your life experiences, and your genetics. More than 20 million people in the United States have depression each year, but you don't have to be a part of this statistic. A negative mind will never give you a positive life. God is your present help, even though life can hurt you so much till you feel there's nothing left, but you have to hold on and stay strong. In case you feel this grey cloud is trying to live rent free over your head, here are some helpful points to help you overcome that feeling:

- **Write down your feelings, your thoughts, your fears, your desires for the future.**
- **Write it down, whether it's in a diary, a note pad or in a journal. Don't worry about spelling or punctuation.**

- **Feel free to draw pictures, write a poem or talk to yourself.**
- **Plan for the future, make short & long term goals**
- **Make a list of all the fun things you want to do as you start to feel better.**
- **Concentrate on the positive things in your life.**
- **Think about or even write about the things you couldn't be doing if you weren't going through your medical treatment. Perhaps you love to read but haven't had time until now.**
- **If you are a working mom, perhaps this is your opportunity to spend more time with your kids.**

Diva, I know you are tired of being tired, but from one survivor to another I am here to tell you to step aside and lean on Jesus because he cares. One of my favorite gospel songstresses' is Mary. Their song *'Can't Give up Now'* is powerful and speaks on the Lord already knowing what you're going through. You can't give up now, because you've came to far from where you started, and God brought you too far to leave you. You may not understand today or tomorrow, but eventually God will Reveal why you went through everything you did.

8

Mirror Check

I don't look like what I've been through; neither do you my fellow Diva. We are strong, because we know our weaknesses. We are beautiful, because we are aware of our flaws. We are fearless, because we learned to recognize, illusion from real. We are wise, because we learned from our mistakes. We are a lover, because we have felt hate. Lastly, we can laugh because we have known sadness. The big question in the chapter is *"What does cancer look like?"*

Of course medically we know it is when abnormal cells divide without control and are able to invade other tissues causing a malignant tumor. However, when your friends, family, coworkers, or even strangers' look at you they are probably shocked that someone like *you* could get cancer. I used to think hmmm that's interesting and what exactly would make me exempt from such an illness? *Why, because you think I'm pretty? I'm in shape? I'm a fashionista? I go to church? My age?* Well the rude awakening to many people who are deaf to the information as it relates to medical studies and statistics, is that it can happen to anyone at any time, at any age, in any tax bracket, or within any race. How about when people really don't know what to say to you in terms of encouragement or support so the first thing they think to acknowledge of you is saying, *"You look great!"* As you respond politely with a smile and sweet *"thank you"*, inside you may be cringing with annoyance and irritation of how someone could hone in on vanity creating the innocent perception of insensitivity to how you may actually *feel* instead; which is much more important for one to inquire about. Looking well and feeling well are two different things. Both are subject matters I did, and still do feel strongly about. Be vocal and inform those around you who may not know what to say or how to approach or acknowledge what you are going through that it's okay to ask questions, and dig a little deeper with concern without coming off as though they are prying. Your makeup, smile, fresh wig, cute clothes, even a pair of new name brand stilettos depending on the occasion are a plus, but for some patients or even post survivors that is only exterior they see, yet on the inside they are fighting the battle of their life…for their life. You have to learn to remain being a victor not a victim during this time and always. I know what it is to be a victim, but I have learned from experience and the Word of God that we can have victory over pain instead of being the victims of it. Remind those around you boldly of Romans 8:37 saying, *"Yet amid all these things we are more than conquerors and gain a surpassing victory through Him who loved us."* (*The Amplified Bible*). The key is the victory is "*through Him.*" If we can learn how to lean on God and receive the strength we need, we truly can "*do all things through Christ who strengthens us*" as stated in Philippians

4:13. Trust your struggle, and know that it is not over until God says it's over.

    We know that friends, family, and colleagues want to help you and be supportive, but some may probably say things and do things that are not helpful, unintentionally. You may be timid or have too sweet of a soul to speak your own truth to correct them at this time, but they have to keep in mind how you feel about yourself is more important than how you look. Nothing is more beautiful than a real smile that has struggled through tears. I'm sure many people feel tongue tied and awkward around cancer patients, because those without faith and God in their hearts focus on *fear vs. faith* getting intimidated with the thought of death. One of the most important messages a friend or loved one can convey to you during this time is their reassurance of them being here for you, and really showing through actions not just words that they love you. Most importantly, God is going to have an important message to preach back to them once it's all over. The phrase *"this is so unfair"* towards you is a lighthearted way making sure you aren't feeling blamed or punished, or even held responsible for the illness. Bad things happen to good people in life, but it's a clear message when said that others recognize it can happen to anyone including themselves. When you have this type of diagnosis, you can't help but feel some element of blame or responsibility, and it's not a positive feeling. When people start lecturing you about how you may have dishonored your parents in life, you were all work and no play, or your food choices were poor, it is phenomenally unhelpful. You don't want to look backwards, you want to look forward. You want to feel hopeful. Those around you should know the importance of meaningful, supportive communication that is going to build you up, not break you down. If people can't do great things, they need to learn how to do small things in a great way. Remember, a simple act of kindness or generosity can change someone's life. Kindness is more than deeds. It is an attitude, an expression, a look, a touch. It is anything that lifts another person.

You may be entering your *"new normal"* right about now adjusting to your pace to approach your finish line. Either way it goes; don't settle for less of a fabulous life than what you had before you were diagnosed. You have to promise yourself that the new normal you create and accept within yourself has to be even better than the old normal that you were comfortable with, yet may have lost sight of when you heard those words, *"you have cancer."* You watched the last dose of chemotherapy drip from the IV into your veins some months ago, and your hair has really started to grow back. Maybe it's curly where it once was straight, or a lot grayer than before, but it's hair. You have eyebrows again. So why are you still so tired? When are you going to feel like you again? "Your body has just been through an enormous assault, and recovery is a huge thing. You're not going to just bounce back right away," says oncologist Marisa Weiss, MD, founder of Breastcancer.org and the author of Living Beyond Breast Cancer. "You've been hit while you're down so many times: with having surgery and anesthesia, perhaps with multiple cycles of chemotherapy, perhaps with radiation." But the day of your last radiation treatment or chemotherapy infusion doesn't mark the end of your journey. Instead, you're about to embark on another avenue, and we aren't talking about Saks 5th my fashionista! This one is all about adjusting to life as a breast cancer survivor.

In many ways, it will be a lot like the life you had before, but in other ways, it will be very different. That's why it's called your "*new normal.*" Your new normal may include making changes in the way you eat, the things you do, the way you treat people, the stress load you choose to take on, and your attitude of gratitude. It's a transition period that can prompt us as survivors to re-examine our life choices. I know I took time to reappraise my job, family relationships, and friendships. I found that I was definitely less tolerant of what we may have put up before being diagnosed. I vowed to start living life more true to who I really was. The new normal comes with having to adapt to new physical sense of self as well as a new sense of emotional vulnerability that may even make you question yourself by saying, "*Am I Crazy?*" To feel exhausted and frustrated at your diminished level of energy is a big cause and effect on you. You may feel angry with many of your "friends" that were nowhere to be found when you needed them most, or ended up disappearing before you crossed the finish line. You could also be concerned about being a burden to your family now. There were times I felt unhappy with my body and the changes due to my treatments and surgery, while playing the waiting game to see my hair grow back on my head, body, and facial attributes. You may find yourself wanting your *"old life"* back, but Diva you must understand that is impossible. You must continue waking up with determination, and going to bed with satisfaction. To believe in you, is to see yourself doing unbelievable things now and in the future.

When completing a mirror check to your life, don't leave out without applying that lip gloss honey! Beauty is more than skin deep, but it doesn't hurt to play with a little makeup to increase your self-confidence. Many patients feel fairly confident about fighting the good fight until they start noticing changes in the mirror. Up until then we don't think about it much, but our bodies, faces, and hair have a lot to do with our identities. They are part of who we are. *What happens when they start to change…who do we become?* In an ideal world, we wouldn't have to worry so much about how we appear to other people, but researchers have found over a number of times that we do base judgments on how people look and sometimes we can become our worse critic. Despite my physical conditions, I still knew how to doll up and look cute! During my summer months in treatment with the sun shining, some days I would put on a nice scarf, apply my makeup to look natural, and go out looking good! Let makeup become your tool, however be conscious of the toxic chemicals that may be in the cosmetics and toiletries you use. Some beauty products contain carcinogens and endocrine-disrupting chemicals that increase breast cancer risk. With a little makeup, you can cover up the flaws that your medical treatment may create on your skin, and still feel confident enough to go to go out to dinner, go to work, or join your friends for some good laughs and fun. If you're suffering from a lack of confidence or just a temporary blues because of your appearance, try these few tips and see if they help. Don't be afraid to seek some extra assistance from your dermatologist or posh makeup artist. This isn't vanity girlfriend; this is about how you feel, and feeling good helps you heal.

- ***Facial Swelling:*** *Use foundation a tad darker than your regular skin tone and blend it on either side of the nose, with a lighter color on the bridge. Try a bronzer along your jaw line to slim the look of your face. Apply cold cucumber to the eye area to reduce swelling, and use eyeliner on the upper lash line to lift the eye. A bit of blush under the eyes can reduce the look of bags.*

- ***Scars:*** *Use a small concealer brush and cover all areas needed using a yellow or golden concealer. Apply foundation or powder over the top.*

- ***Pimples:*** *A yellow-based concealer applied sparingly is best—work from the center out, and blend well at the edges. Apply after you apply foundation.*

- ***Under-Eye Circles:*** *Use a concealer with a warm (pink) undertone to counteract the blueness. Apply moisturizer first, and then apply concealer underneath the lashes.*

- ***Loss of Lashes:*** *Line the upper lash line with a brownish-black soft tip pencil or pen, smudge it, and then apply mascara to the lashes you have left. Avoid using a curler or waterproof formulas, as they can increase lash loss. When your lashes are completely gone, use liner except on special occasions, when you may want to apply fake lashes. Just be careful of the chemicals in the glue.*

- ***Loss of Eyebrows:*** *Determine a shape for your brows—using a stencil is the best way to get your desired shape (rounded or angular, for instance). Use eyebrow makeup shades that most closely match your natural hair color. Use a pencil to dot along the brow line, creating the line of your eyebrow, then take your brow brush and apply the shadow or brow color over the pencil line and throughout* the brow area. Brush through both pencil and color to blend.

- ***Pale, Ashy Skin***: Use a bronzer. Test a little on your skin before applying all over to make sure the color matches. Those with cool, pinkish tones do better with shades that have a touch of pink, while those with yellow or golden tones do well with gold, tan, or brown bronzers. Warmer olive tones should choose bronzers with amber or honey undertones, and women of color may want to choose bronzers with burgundy or copper undertones.

"I'm not trying to look perfect. I just want to feel better, look great, know I'm healthy, and be able to rock any outfit I choose!"

- *Unknown*

9

Pink Boas & Bones Aches

The meaning of the color pink is unconditional love and nurturing. In color psychology pink is a sign of hope. It is a positive color inspiring warm and comforting feelings, a sense that everything will be okay. As it relates to breast cancer awareness it is a color of being intuitive and insightful, while showing tenderness and kindness with its empathy and sensitivity. God's plans will always be greater and more beautiful than all your disappointments especially during this time. I understand that some days you will have to create your own sunshine, but to be the best you have to be able to handle the worst. As many as 2.3 million American women have survived or are currently fighting, and we all have a story to tell. There are many organizations all over the world that support and celebrate the unity of fighting against breast cancer and finding a cure. Some of the major conglomerate organizations such as Avon, Susan G. Komen, and the American Cancer Society host annual walks and runs to make strides against this disease which has affected so many of our family members, friends, and even friends of friends. As a survivor, I have participated in three walks thus far with my Mom, God-Mom, and my God-Sisters supporting me and the pink ribbon cause. I remember my first walk in May

2011, not only did I raise over $400, but being there in the present was so empowering and emotionally overwhelming with feelings of excitement, joy, laughter, sadness, and a spirit of gratitude to be alive and apart of such a wonderful day. If you're yet to participate in a walk/run, the city of Chicago transforms into a sea of pink ribbons with participants wearing creative pink attire. Seeing countless number of encouraging signs, and the enormous amount of support from individuals and businesses presented me with the *wow factor*, warming my heart. For the first time I saw the magnitude of what I fought through, my story, my testimony, and realizing I wasn't in this alone. God allowed me to go through this storm to test me and build me up, so therefore I felt a renewed energy from within. It was as though every survivor I met that day was a long lost sister I had never met. They knew the struggle, understood the lingo, and could celebrate the fact that we beat it before it beat us. So remember that as you engage in your annual October breast cancer awareness activities, Sunday brunches, and walks for the Cause, take a moment and pause for the #1 cause–**YOU!**

"Wherever there is a human in need, there is an opportunity for kindness and to make a difference." — Kevin Heath

Knowledge is power and power produces survivors. Some men or women diagnosed are so consumed with the fear factor they try to avoid or decide to decline receiving the medical treatment recommended by the doctor. So many beautiful, vibrant women are dying senselessly of this disease, losing yet another young mother, sister, or friend especially due to fear is now totally unacceptable, and needs to cease especially within the African American communities. Breast cancer is treatable and the fear associated with it is fully conquerable! Divas, you can fight it and win! So you have to say it loud and proud with me that THE DEATHS STOP HERE! Before you start tying those pink ribbons and slipping on your pink fall fashions in support of finding a cure, think about the lives you hope to help save–including *yours*! Shift your focus to YOU! Breast cancer is the most common cancer among Black women and is the second leading cause of cancer deaths exceeded only by lung cancer. It's time to go beyond the traditional norms of general awareness programs. If the agenda doesn't address moving you from fear to power, it needs an upgrade. Because Black women are more often diagnosed with this terrible disease at a younger age (under the age of 40), experience more aggressive tumors, and are more likely to pass away from this than white women even though more white women get the disease. It's time to make a lifelong commitment and become an advocate for your own body. Your diagnosis past or present does not discriminate, and it strikes every single day on women across the globe. Therefore it's time to be aware of its impact throughout the whole year! No matter your age, your treatment plan depends on many factors, such as the type of breast cancer you have and the characteristics of the tumor. Your overall health and other health conditions you may have also play a role in your treatment plan. For example, if you have heart disease, some medications can cause more harm than good. All of these things help tailor your treatment plan.

Younger women going through this struggle have special concerns about early menopause, and loss of fertility due to treatment. I am yet to bear any children of my own; however I believe and trust God when the time comes that I won't have any conceiving complications. Due to my age of being twenty-six, in July 2010 my oncologist recommended that I complete the IVF egg preservation process prior to beginning chemo. That was a surgical day procedure that was harmless, so thankfully I now have four healthy *young* eggs waiting for me on ice worst case scenario whenever I am ready. So my biological clock can tick all it wants too now! There are specific medical treatment options for different types of non-invasive and invasive breast cancers. One of the following stages may sound very familiar to you: *Ductal carcinoma in situ (DCIS, stage 0), Early breast cancer (stages I and II), Local advanced/inflammatory breast cancer (stage III), and Metastatic breast cancer (stage IV)*. According to studies of Susan G. Komen; treatment for ductal carcinoma in situ (DCIS) which is a non-invasive breast cancer, involves surgery and possibly radiation therapy and/or tamoxifen, which is proving to be very effective in preventing a recurrence in patients who are hormone-receptor positive. Treatment for invasive breast cancer usually involves some combination of surgery, radiation therapy, chemotherapy, hormone therapy and/or targeted therapy. The order of the therapies and the specific treatments depend on the cancer stage and the characteristics of the actual tumor. There are approximately sixty prescription drugs approved by the Food and Drug Administration (FDA) for breast cancer, but sadly still no cure. The list includes generic and brand names. Medicines are used to treat you, and also help relieve side effects of treatment. A combination of medicines is typically used to treat you at this time, especially if you have to undergo chemotherapy. The number of cycles of treatment will depend on the medicines that are used and how the medicines are given.

Stage is usually expressed as a number on a scale of 0 through IV. Stage 0 describes non-invasive cancers that remain within their original location and stage IV describes invasive cancers that have spread outside the breast to other parts of the body. Thankfully I was diagnosed in the early stages being IIB *triple negative*. So I gave my consent to take part in a clinical research trial that based on my demographics I was eligible to partake in at that time. The study had a high survival rate from others involved nationwide, so with careful consideration and information provided by my oncologist I agreed and signed on the dotted line. I was given 4 cycles of Adriamycin, Cytoxan, and Avastin through IV infusion. Then the second part of my chemotherapy clinical trial included 4 cycles of Taxol and Avastin. I was driven back to the hospital within 24-hours after my chemo infusion so my nurse could give me a Neulasta shot; which is a prescription medication that helps reduce a patient's risk of infection by supporting the body's natural defenses. It does this by boosting the number of infection-fighting white blood cells. I did not suffer any intense complications from my chemo thankfully. I did acquire a sore throat at one point which was not good to have during treatment so my doctor was notified, my appetite was very minimal for a longtime, taste buds changed, nails turned a little black, heavy fatigue, and overall a feeling that is similar to flu and cold symptoms throughout the full week after my infusion. It would shut me down to the point I barely had the strength to glance at my phone or walk downstairs for a change of scenery while at my Mom's house. While everyone else was enjoying their summer fun, all I could do is sleep the day away waiting for the heavy symptoms to wear off. During my first infusion summer of July 2010, I was nervous and scared from the poor choice of information overload off the internet. However, I still managed to check into the chemo room with my Mom looking my best with my cute hoop earrings, a pink ribbon designed tank top, a pink ribbon bracelet with *hope, faith, and love* inscribed on it, makeup looking flawless, all while not truly knowing what to expect. After watching DVD's and reading books to get through five long hours, I finally finished my first chemo treatment of many more to come. *Yay me right?* Well, I felt a little *"tipsy"* which the nurses like calling each infusions your *"cocktail"* due to the after effect, thankfully it eventually wore off. I was prescribed anti-nausea pills to help prevent the need to vomit from stomach discomfort from the heavy meds, they worked great, however I lost a lot of weight since I could not eat like I was used to eating due to loss of appetite. I started at 158 pounds and dropped down to 144 pounds at one point, all my vivacious curves disappeared momentarily, but on the positive note I looked like a slim gem from *Vogue* magazine with my new love for grapes, and managing with small baby bites of my food! Four long months of my life sitting in the chemo room letting medications drip slowly from an IV into my vein, while my Mom kept me company never missing an appointment. Giving me her tender loving care as the seasons changed outside the same window of our private room. Adriamycin has a nickname of "red devil." That's the drug that not only has strong effects of nausea, vomiting, diarrhea, and loss of appetite occurring; but also is responsible of temporary hair loss and nail changes. It's a very dangerous drug apparently for others to come in contact me, my oncology Nurse Josie had long surgical type gloves on, eye wear, and a cape over her uniform. Very intimidating and scary to know something so harmful is being injected as a poison to your healthy cells. The taxol medication was the second part of my chemo infusion which was weekly for six weeks in a row and more manageable to handle and stomach. However, it took two rounds for me to realize where this new tingling/burning sensation on my hands and feet was coming from! Eeekkkk! That was the worse form of punishment; I could not stand for long periods of time, or even walk my dog without my feet feeling like they were on fire. I'm telling you the simple day to day things we all take for granted! I would have to run cool water on them, use a Eucerin lotion, and just stay put on my sofa the rest of the day with my feet up to keep the circulation going, which that part wasn't so bad!

Heal through exercise, don't sweat the small stuff, and keep in mind if it doesn't challenge you, it doesn't change you. After surviving your diagnosis and treatment, you may wonder if you'll ever regain your strength. Whether or not you were able to stay active during your treatment, regular physical activity will be an important part of your recovery plan. Currently as a four-year survivor, I still suffer from bone aches and joint pain most likely attributing to IV taxol treatment I received. I am thirty years old, and sometimes after a full day out and about my legs get achy and I have to rub them or elevate them to rest and increase circulation. It still can get frustrating, because I am young and some days I feel aged beyond my years. The wear and tear of my treatment is having a long term effect on me after all it seems, but I keep rocking my stilettos most days. Having dance as a first love, I use a few days within the week to get my heart rate up by shaking my tail feather right there in my living room, without having to make a drive to see a trainer. It gets the job done just like a paid gym membership would! Many breast cancer survivors say that getting and staying active has played a big role in getting their lives back, and I will definitely agree. During your recovery and healing process exercise plays a big part in your well-being now and in the future. Regular exercise builds strength and endurance, giving you more energy to do the things you enjoy. It helps restore physical function lost to inactivity or medical treatments. And research demonstrates a strong link between an active lifestyle and a brighter future for every survivor. Some main points relating to regular exercise benefits is the ability to help restore a normal range of motion, especially for shoulder mobility after your surgery. Better physical function, reduced fatigue, and bodily pain are also benefits of increased physical activity. Despite all the pros to exercising there are some concerns that cause some survivors not to get heavily involved due to lack of information about safe and effective exercise that won't put them at risk for lymphedema. Recent studies have shown that neither aerobic exercise nor resistance training is linked to developing or worsening of breast cancer-related lymphedema. Better yet, one study found that women who followed a slow, progressive strength-training program lowered their risk of developing lymphedema by 35 percent; women who had at least five lymph nodes removed and started lifting weights reduced their risk by 70 percent. Not only is strength-training ideal for preventing lymphedema, it also helps build strong bones, good posture, and overall strength. When I exercise or even fly on airplanes, I still wear my therapy arm sleeve to make sure my lymph nodes circulate my blood properly without any discomfort. We all have to take care of our bodies; it's the only place we have to live in. Talk with your doctor first, work with a certified trainer experienced with designing a well-balanced exercise program tailored to your needs, goals, and interests. Be sure to start slowly, be patient, and gather support with a community of women that know what you are going through. So think about how far you've come today, and how much further you'll go tomorrow. You are going to want to give up, but don't.

There is always a chance to celebrate, since celebration is a state of mind, and when being aware; a state of being. Oprah Winfrey once said, *"The more you praise and celebrate your life, the more there is in life to celebrate."* So Diva I say to you loud and proud now is the time to celebrate yourself! You have been through the fire and back, and you are still here on this Earth to make in a difference, while standing before many with the strength and resilience you never knew you had within. Celebrate your life, because sometimes people forget their own greatness. Pastor Joel Osteen says, *"When nobody else celebrates you, learn to celebrate yourself. When nobody else compliments you, learn to compliment yourself. It's not up to other people to keep you encouraged. It's up to you! Encouragement should come from the inside."* You are surviving at this very moment, so it is important to honor your inner radiance right now! Not tomorrow, not next week, next month, or wait until next year; tomorrow isn't promised, so tame the insidious voices that make you feel worthless or small and celebrate your own magnificence every day. I suggest finding something to celebrate every moment, and in this case let's focus on self-love. Turn your awareness towards yourself and celebrate your energy and being. No matter how good or bad you think life is, wake up each day and be thankful for life. As you and I both know there people like us fighting to survive. Since we never know what will happen next, we have to be thankful and carry a spirit of gratitude for all we have. *"Giving thanks always for all things unto God and the Father in the name of our Lord Jesus Christ."* Ephesians 5:20. Sure, we can always have more, but by the same token we could always have less. I know our shoe closets never can have enough shimmer in them, and I'm sure we all would love a new flashy sports car to drive around town to valet at the city's hottest restaurant or lounge. But, reality sets in and helps you realize that the best things in life aren't even things. You're not just simply to be thankful one day a year. One day is not long enough to thank God for all that He's given you. His blessings come daily. Psalm 68:19 says, *"Blessed be the Lord, Who daily loadeth us with benefits..."* Every day God has brand-new blessings for you, and every day ought to find you thanking God. Every prayer that you pray ought to be salted with thanks. Our gratitude is a healing force from within our souls, and should be pervasive, perpetual, proper, pleasurable, and possible. Thankful people are happy people. *"Well,"* you say, *"if I had something to be thankful for, I'd be happy."* You have missed the point! You do have something to be thankful for. You have life. If you are a Christian, you have Christ. You may say, *"But my circumstances are not good."* The apostle Paul was in prison when he wrote this letter to the Ephesians, yet he was rejoicing in the Lord. Gratefulness turned his prison to a palace, but ungratefulness can turn your palace to a prison. I'm telling you, the attitude of gratitude will change your life. I don't care how bad, difficult, dark, or mysterious things get medically or personally; take the ultimate step of faith and say, *"God, you're greater than this, and I thank you."*

Live for today, laugh for tomorrow, and love forever. When you live for today, despite your circumstances you don't let the negatives define your life and who you are. Focus on living, not cancer. If you want to go skydiving, travel the world, be a Rock Star for a day, or take a sushi making class, seize the day, time is too precious to waste. All you need in the world is love and laughter. Laughter has tremendous power on healing and is an instant vacation from the mundane reality of worries or stress, especially as it relates to the effects of dealing with breast cancer. It is a good cure for all that may be bad, and it is a great way to show the world truly how strong you are. If I had a flower for every time my Mother or friends made me laugh during some of my toughest days when I didn't feel like feeling, I would have a garden to walk in forever. In the words of Audrey Hepburn, "*I love people who make me laugh. I honestly think it's the thing I like most, to laugh. It cures a multitude of ills. It's probably the most important thing in a person.*" Tough times don't last, tough people do. A recent study found that 5-year old children laugh up to 400 times a day! In this case it's the kids who can teach us a thing or two! So, start counting how often you laugh. Good humor is tonic for the mind and body. It is the best antidote for anxiety and depression. It is a business asset, which attracts and keeps friends. It lightens human burdens, and is the direct route to serenity and contentment. Embrace the hearts that will love you at your worst, and arms that will hold you at your weakest. Love is infectious and the greatest healing energy, which leads us to believe that love, conquers all. So with that being said, you only live once? False. You live every day. You only die once.

Gratitude unlocks the fullness of life. It turns what we have into enough, and more. It turns denial into acceptance, chaos into order; confusion into clarity...Gratitude makes sense of our past, brings peace for today and creates a vision for tomorrow. — Melodie Beattie

10

Back on Your Own

Adjusting to life after going through so much medically can be a long, arduous road. Many women struggle to return to life as they knew it before their diagnosis only to find that their definition of *"normal"* is no longer relevant. Along with dealing with the effects of breast cancer the heightened sense of vulnerability and a diminished sense of control will come. It's normal for us all to have moments of uncertainty and fear even after treatment, however don't let it control or consume your second chance at life. Once the main part of your treatment is over, you might feel relieved. You don't have to visit the hospital as often, you can begin to recover from the side effects of treatment, and you may start to think about hosting a holiday party or going back to work. Going through your intense medical treatment may have stopped you from doing some of your usual activities. These might be hobbies, seeing relatives and friends, or things like cooking, modeling, or photography that used to be a regular part of your life before being diagnosed. After treatment is over, I encourage you to start doing these again, though you need to take things slowly at first. Questions of *"Am I cured? Will I have a recurrence? Will I survive a recurrence? What happens now?"* may start to ponder in your thoughts. Even though they are unanswerable, that's when you have to place a deposit within your faith bank account allowing God to drive while you ride shot gun! One of the most common feelings you may experience or be currently experiencing after your medical journey has ended is loneliness, and the sense of being back on your own. It is an unfortunate reality that having cancer can change relationships. The impact on family and friends cannot be overestimated. It is likely that some friendships, even old ones, may be lost due to this stress; while others will be forged and strengthened. It can be a rude awakening to see how fast everyone who was concerned about you can return to their former lives. You may also notice how those that were too *"busy"* to stop and take a minute to care about someone other than themselves in the beginning, will now resurrect to send a well wish since they heard through the grapevine that you're on the road to recovery and doing well. There is a true saying that goes, *"It is during the worst times of your life that you will get to see the true colors of the people who say they care for you."* A common complaint of survivors is the apparent belief of those around them that, once the last treatment is over, the cancer patient life is over. Those who have never had to deal with a life threatening diagnosis tend to assume that on your last day of treatment you have reached the finish line, and now you can celebrate picking up your life exactly where you left off as though you didn't miss a beat. Reality is quite different. The effects of therapy don't necessarily stop when therapy stops. Alert Diva in distress!

From the moment of diagnosis, through all the ups and downs of treatment, a Diva like you is prone to operate in crisis mode. It may have even become your standard way of functioning, so by switching to a day-to-day life without crisis can actually feel wrong. Some divas are able to maintain most of their normal life routines and insist that breast cancer is a disruption that can be managed. You may be one of those superwomen who appeared to have no problems during your treatment, however after treatment created more time to think and reflect on the illness you survived through, which allows your emotions to finally catch up. Either way, it can all lead to astonishment now leaving you to feel overwhelmed with emotions and unable to function. A friend I know who also is a survivor would call her medical oncologist when she could barely get out of bed in the morning and found herself weeping uncontrollably. She explained that she had never before felt so out of control and that she overwhelmed by her feelings so it would cause her to cry and feel like she was going crazy. I know for a fact, that I struggled with many problems that were new to me and that were directly related to my diagnosis and treatment. I was exhausted many days and would get very frustrated with my diminished level of energy. Surgery, radiation therapy, and chemotherapy as we know are physically grueling, leaving most of us with little emotional and physical energy to spare. You may expect to recover rapidly, but you may still find yourself feeling unwell and exhausted for a frustratingly long time. I am currently a four-year survivor going on forever, and still suffer from fatigue having to listen to my body and know when it is time to rest. When I'm down somehow my Shih Tzu Nino knows his Mommy is tired, he is a great nap buddy and we both have a love for good rest and relaxation! *Sleeping Beauty* is my Alpha Kappa Alpha, Sorority Inc. given line-name, so it was pre-destined I guess! When my energy level starts to lessen my sweetheart takes good care of me. We found that his delicious homemade baked kale chips which are a great source of iron really help bring me back to life! However, you may go through a period being angry with your *"friends"* who were not there for you when you needed them most. Friendship is not about whom you've known the longest. It's about who walked into your life saying, "I'm here for you."…and proved it. Even though you may feel hurt, you must still forgive others not because they deserve forgivingness, but because you deserve peace.

I also went through moments during treatment and afterwards that I was unhappy with my body and the changes due to my treatments including surgery. I hated waiting for my hair to grow even though I enjoyed the new texture and the easy wake up and go, however some days the imagination of my mind would get busy to the point I would say I felt *"fat and ugly"* just to release the built up emotional tension I had some days. We are all prone to experiencing these same negative emotions, but you have to know how to control them as well so they don't get out of hand, and lead to heavy depression. Tony Wagner once said, *"Isolation is the enemy of improvement."* The sense of isolation may be made worse if you find it difficult to talk about yourself and your emotions. It can be hard to talk to others about how you really feel, especially if you sense that they think you should be able to get on with life now and *"feel fine"*. For some people their treatment may have been aimed at taking precautionary measures, so they lean on hope to put it all behind them. Others may have been told that even in remission the cancer is likely to return, but no one can say for sure if and when this will happen. Uncertainty is one of the hardest things to deal with and can cause a lot of tension. You may feel irritable, angry and frightened. You may even feel conflicted as you now embrace finishing your treatment, but you know there are others close to you who may still be going through treatment or who sadly lost their battle fighting their fight. It's difficult to make plans when you don't know what lies ahead. And even if you ask your doctors what's likely to happen, you may find that their answers are vague because they can't say for sure. This uncertainty can be very hard to cope with, especially when you're trying to get back to a normal routine. Optimism will always lift your spirits.

Challenge yourself to focus your attention and your efforts on understanding your survivorship. Healing is not an overnight process. It is a daily cleansing of pain; it is a daily healing of your life. Preparing yourself for the post treatment period of dealing with the effects whether it's by educating yourself, or allowing your doctor to assist you with medical advice with the same detail, empathy, and attention that was given in earlier explanations of diagnosis and treatment planning is a very important part of your recovery. A general rule of thumb is that it takes approximately as long as the total duration of treatment to really feel well again. Don't allow what you have been through to diminish your sense of self-worth. You are a Superwoman now in the eyes of so many, you just have to value and believe it yourself! Allow your recovery and life in post treatment to change you in ways that strengthen your relationships not strain them. Don't be afraid to open yourself to new ideas and experiences verses only clinging to things that are familiar. During my recovery I created my very first scrapbook full of pictures, medical notes, affirmations, and lots of love. Despite the challenges, it's possible to rebuild a really good life after such a hard journey, so be in love with your life… every minute of it. There are different ways of learning to live with uncertainty. Try taking control of the things that you do have control over. Think about making some changes to your lifestyle and environment - perhaps to your diet, or your work-life balance. Also consider using complementary therapies whereas therapists usually work with the person as a whole, not just part of the body where the cancer was. This is called a holistic approach, and is something good healthcare practitioners also do that can possibly help you in your daily life mentally and emotionally. Embracing your normal activities and creating a new routine is the best way to help yourself feel better about you and your new life, especially as you regain strength and are able to do more overtime.

I remember a bittersweet epiphany I had after becoming so comfortable and somewhat co-dependent on all the assistance and care I was openly receiving from my Mother and those that would help when they could. As I was back on my own, I realized I now had to clean my own condo, cook my own meals again, and walk my own dog all by myself! It was funny, yet somewhat of a struggle regaining my independency, even though I told my Mom from the beginning I was not moving out of my condo so she could be a 24/7 caretaker having me at what I like to call her home "the Headquarters." I needed to be in my own space to maintain my level of normalcy. During the first few rounds of heavy chemo I stayed at her home until we both adjusted, and when I was feeling better once it wore off prior to my next round I would come back to my condo (which was only 10 minutes away) and be able to maintain on my own. With a little compromise and understanding, it worked. What I realized over time was although I was now Miss Independent again; I knew I was never alone. The real work is just beginning, and is up to only you to maintain your well-being and manage your health. Healthy eating, exercising, vitamins to boost your immune system to maintain healthy formation of your cells, staying on track scheduling your post-survival doctor visits, no smoking, keeping your stress levels low, living "green" if you can, getting your appropriate sleep, and making sure you still regularly perform your own self breast exams will all be a part of your new regiment of life assisting with preventing a reoccurrence. One full year after your diagnosis, I want you to feel strong, healthy and optimistic about your future. You deserve to enjoy your family and the simple things that you once never noticed before. Get your fire back! It's not over until God says it's over. Start believing again. Start dreaming again. Start pursuing what God put in your heart. I'm cheering for you!

"Change is no longer a choice, but an imperative to survive."

– Elsie A. Harry

11
Live Out Loud

You cannot be who you are and who you used to be at the same time. It's a brand new you, on a brand new journey. It's time to live and celebrate your life in a big way once you've finished your treatments. Regardless of age being younger or older, if you've always had the desire to travel the world and explore the unseen then go for it. Plan a getaway for the weekend, or plan a fabulous trip you've been putting off. This can be a road trip, or a cruise, or anything that excites and thrills you. Plan a party of some kind, rewarding yourself for successfully completing your treatments. You are a survivor, you deserve it! *Have you ever wanted to ride in a hot air balloon, learn to salsa dance, become a long-distance bike rider or embark your dream adventure?* After a breast cancer diagnosis you may feel the need to want to "take back" your body by testing your abilities and erasing limitations. Reclaim your strength and identity by taking on physical challenges. Many individuals choose to use their experience to push for increased research, more comprehensive legislative policy, or educate the public through outreach events or media coverage especially to inform young women like us. You have a voice, and you are free to use it in the best way you see fit. My personal story of celebration has been an annual out of the country family trip with just my Mom and me. We tend to travel every year around April, which is the month I was diagnosed back in 2010. Thus far we have been able to enjoy Cancun, Bahamas, and Aruba. My skin was very sensitive to the sun after completing radiation a few months prior, so Diva make sure you wear your sunscreen despite wanting to layout in the sun and tan. I learned the hard way that it's better to be safe than sorry, especially after being exposed to so much medically. Each trip has been memorable in its own special way, so I look forward to the adventures that wait. Truth is told, even if the way we celebrate changes as the years go by, as long as we have each other that's a celebration enough for me.

Rock your runway of life, *girlfriend*! You have to remind yourself and others that today is going to be the first day of the best day of your life, and they haven't seen anything yet! One of my favorite gospel artist Donald Lawrence has a song called *"The best is yet to come."* It speaks to your soul about not giving up, and keep looking up, because there is a master plan in store for you. If you just make it through, God's going to really blow your mind, and make it worth your time for all of the trouble you've been through. The best seems double just for you, so be confident and embrace the new you. Too many days are wasted comparing ourselves to others and wishing to be something we aren't. Everybody has their own strengths and weaknesses, and it is only when you accept everything you are, and you aren't that you will truly succeed. Confidence is not about being proud of yourself; it is about believing in yourself… it makes you beautiful. I've always been the type of Diva to do what I want, and say what I want, because those that mind don't matter, and those that matter don't mind! I encourage you always act like you are wearing an invisible crown. It is so important to express yourself through words, writing, dance, music, or whichever outlet that allows you to uncork your feelings and emotions. Every being in this World communicates in some fashion, even animals. And the more complex the form of communication is, you will find more complex relationships as well. Human speech is the most complicated form of communication in the world. We have so many ways to express ideas, feelings, dreams, suggestions, thoughts, intents, love, rage, desire, and so forth. So it is important that you learn to express yourself. You must learn to convey your thoughts, ideas, dreams, ambitions, hopes and emotions to those that you share a relationship with. Your inability to do so, will damage your relationships, so strive to be known as an intelligent woman, a courageous woman, a loving woman, a woman who teaches by being. God is working in your life, so go forward to create inspired healing, wellness and have live out loud joy.

"I believe that life is a prize. But to live doesn't mean you're alive." – Nicki Minaj

12

Praise & Purpose

Praise and Purpose are two of the most important acts of service we can fulfill in our lifetime here on Earth. According to Wikipedia, *"Praise is the act of making positive statements about a person, object or idea, wither public or privately."* Praise is typically, but not exclusively, earned relative to achievement and accomplishment. Purpose is the reason for which something is done or created or for which something exists. Life is not a dress rehearsal. So many of us float through life thinking the life we are living must be as good as it gets. For many of you, it is not. There is more. YOU have a purpose. With both words used in the context of your survival, you are now responsible in fulfilling your purpose through your praise. You may ask, *"Well how does that happen?"* There is healing in praise, and God's sunlight in the heart. It keeps the heart pure and the eye clear. Praise is essential to the knowledge of God and His will. The renewed strength of your life is the strength of your song, and your song can help you fulfill your purpose. As a survivor and human being on this Earth, I believe my purpose is to be a joy into the lives of those around me. To be inspiring through the love I share, laughter I bring, and the life through Christ in which I live. So often, we take the little things for granted. We act as if this is the warm up for the big show, *well guess what?* This is the BIG show, *Hunnie*! So many people live life never reaching their full potential because of fear of the unknown. We all at some point in our lives have complained about not having this or not having that, when we should be simply grateful for the fact we are still breathing. There are some patients struggling with complications of their diagnosis that hardly can breathe at this moment. *If you were told you only had a few weeks to live, would you be happy with the life you've lived?* If your answer is no, then it's time to start thinking about your purpose. You only get one life and you don't have to live it in a box. You can live the life you create, but it will require some faith, action and guts. So I challenge you to start thinking about your life. *What is your DREAM? What would you LOVE to do? What are you GOOD at? What is your PURPOSE? What would make you HAPPY?* Think about it. Write it down. Develop it. Do it. Whatever you want your story to be, live it, and trust that I know the best is within you. You just have to believe it for yourself.

If you wake up every day with the motive and mission to make a difference in the life of everyone you encounter, you will start to see and feel the difference of how people perceive and gravitate to you wanting more of you. Everyone does not get to experience that positive change from the inside out in such a big way like we as survivors do. Luke 17:19 says, *"I Am A Living Testimony."* Life is brimming with possibilities, its where *"What if?"* runs away

"*Why Not?*" It's taking the trail less traveled to a miraculous testimony so you can share your story and live to inspire since you now have true life through brand new eyes. I am one hundred percent a different woman then I was four years ago. I'm stronger, more confident, and so much more grateful for the people in my inner circle that never wavered with their support. God has indeed fulfilled so much through my pink ribbon journey. He transformed me. I give thanks and praise to Him for the good purposes in my life. I can't help but say: *"Thank you, Lord, for this was your good pleasure."* (Matthew 11:26) A remarkably important way of giving back as a survivor is through the sense of meaning and purpose in wanting to do something for others. When another patient has the ability to see and talk with someone who has lived through their story and beat the odds surviving breast cancer, which is a more tangible sign that they too can and will survive. It can be more important than any words of wisdom or encouragement from a doctor. It is truly a gift of hope and can be given only by someone who has been there and truly can relate. Hope is so important early on, and to give back as a volunteer, by your own presence now, makes a new patient feel like, *"If you made it, I can, too."* The other side of giving back and paying it forward is the feeling of reward of having helped someone else with the same problem. I have been a match for 1-on-1 cancer support as a volunteer with the Imerman Angels organization three times so far, and I can truly say that I got as much out of the encounter as the patient did and they are now survivors as well. I suggest to those who are currently still in treatment on their road to recovery, to continue focusing on your own needs for now. No matter how you feel… get up, dress up, show up, and never give up! Your season will come, be strong enough to wait for it.

13
Facts of Life

Breast cancer prevention needs to become a shared conversation among women of all ages, as it can strike at any age and is generally more aggressive when diagnosed in women under the age of fifty. Health is the first of life, wealth is the next of life, character's courage is the best of life, respect is must in life, turning is the test of life, and God's blessing is the crest of life. Happiness is the perfume of life; truth is the search of life, while death is the rest of life. Alex Hailey once said, *"You have to deal with the fact that your life is your life."* I must agree. We have gotten this far, now it's time to face all the facts and be sure that you have the knowledge to move forward successfully carrying your survivor torch lighting the way for others to eventually follow. As we know my self-breast exam before I got out of bed that cold morning in December of 2009 changed my life. Many young women are not aware of their risks. Genes play a role in breast cancer risk for some women; lifestyles changes cut risk for many others. The U.S. Preventative Services Task Force confused a number of women across the country when it announced three years ago that women between the ages of 40 and 49 should not get routine mammograms for early breast cancer detection—something at odds with the American Cancer Society's stance that annual mammograms should begin at age 40. *So which advice should you follow?* New research nets some clear advice. Two new reports in the journal Annals of Internal Medicine finds that the necessity of annual screenings really depends on who you are. If you're at a high risk for breast cancer for any reason, then starting annual mammograms at age forty is a good choice. If you're not, then less frequent screenings may be your best bet. This is great information, *but what about us?* The young and fabulous Divas that are continued statistical proof that *"young women"* under the age of forty can get it too? "Unfortunately, college-age women generally do not consider themselves at risk for breast cancer," said Dr. Mercier to news-medical.net. "However, there are several risk factors that contribute to the development of breast cancer that need to be understood early in life to prevent the development of breast cancer down the road." If you are currently in your early twenties or know someone who needs to become aware of some key risk factors associated with breast cancer; tell them to check their family tree, including keeping your weight in normal range (body mass index under 25), being physically active (at least 30 minutes a day of moderate-intensity exercise), minimizing alcohol intake (one drink a day or less), and don't smoke. Overweight, inactivity and alcohol all increase risk for breast cancer, and smoking increases risk in some women. Anne McTiernan, M.D., Ph.D. a member of the Center's Public Health Sciences Division and author of "Breast Fitness" says for young women: Breast-feed your babies for as long as possible. Women who breast-feed their babies for at least a year in total have a reduced risk of developing breast cancer, so you can keep that in mind now and in the future.

Diva, we always use and hear the word mammogram and screening, *but what do they mean to our health?* Mammograms can be used to check for breast cancer in women who have no signs or symptoms of the disease. This type of mammogram is called a screening mammogram. Screening mammograms usually involve two x-ray pictures, or images, of each breast. The x-ray images make it possible to detect tumors that cannot be felt. Screening mammograms can also find *micro calcifications,* which are tiny deposits of calcium that sometimes indicate the presence of breast cancer. Mammograms can also be used to check for breast cancer after a lump or other sign or symptom of the disease has been found. This type of mammogram is called a diagnostic mammogram. Besides a lump, signs of breast cancer can include breast pain, thickening of the skin of the breast, nipple discharge, or a change in breast size or shape; however, these signs may also be signs of benign conditions, so it's always best to pay attention to your body, and notify your doctor of any irregular changes. Now we ask are screening and diagnostic mammograms different? Diagnostic mammography takes longer than screening mammography, because more x-rays are needed to obtain views of the breast from several angles. The technician may magnify a suspicious area to produce a detailed picture that can help the doctor make an accurate diagnosis. You find that some young women who exercise regularly, don't drink or smoke, and may even be a vegetarian for ten plus years still became a part of our pink ribbon sisterhood while being under the age of 35. Many young women diagnosed, such as me made the decision to undergo genetic testing. In some of those cases, many are unaware that they have been carrying a hereditary BRCA1 or BRCA2 gene mutation, which dramatically increases one's risk. Thankfully, my test came back negative with no genetic trace. Overall doll, be informed and be your own judge. Don't let other people scare you from getting screened or seeing a doctor. When breast cancers are discovered at an early, "localized" stage and treated (the current standard of treatment for early-stage breast cancer is lumpectomy followed by radiation), there is a 97 percent rate of five-year survival. I can't wait to celebrate my five-year survival! That will be such a weight off my shoulders to know I finally made it to the statistical safety mark! The Diva who religiously complains that her mammogram hurts might be a *"Negative Nancy,"* but better to be informed than left in the dark, because once again, **early detection saves lives**.

"Chemoprevention, which is the reversal, suppression or prevention of cancer cell development by edible phytochemicals (fruit and vegetable compounds) and dietary modification is now considered to be an effective, inexpensive, acceptable and accessible approach to cancer control and management (according to World Health Organization, 2011)." Diet and nutrition play a fundamental role in the way in which our bodies respond to and recover from our diagnosed treatment. Believe it or not there are high levels of *carotenoids* which are nutrients found in fruits and vegetables that aid in promoting cancer cell death, preventing cancer cells developing new blood vessels, reducing blood sugar levels that cancer cells need for energy and growth, and boost the effectiveness of the immune system. Carotenoids are the micronutrients in fruits and vegetables that give them their vibrant orange, yellow, and red colors. Foods that are good sources of carotenoids include carrots, sweet potatoes, spinach, kale, red peppers, and winter squash. Having higher circulating blood-carotenoid levels may be particularly protective against breast cancers that do not need estrogen to grow, such as being triple-negative. It's exciting that fruits and vegetables may help prevent breast cancer, but we don't want to give high-risk women a false sense that if they eat right they don't have to be vigilant about screening. The foods that your mother always told you are good for you, truly are good for you. A treat here and there is okay in moderation, but let's learn to say no to the refined sugars, carbonated drinks, artificial foods, and processed fried foods. Vitamins I have found personally to be beneficial in aiding to my survivorship includes vitamin D, vitamin E, CoQ10, Cell food drops, Bitter Melon Extract, Graviola,

Red Raspberry Complex, and a baby aspirin from time to time. Feel free to research and look into those for yourself or for others you may know who would find these additional supplements to be beneficial to their health regiment.

Healing is not an event, but a journey with many stops and starts along the way. The thought of living through the physical and emotional toll of having to deal with a reoccurrence is unbearable and can be traumatic to any survivor's mental state. Many young women who've been diagnosed believe they'll be safer and spare themselves the stress of future treatment if they have both breasts removed, even if their surgeon isn't recommending it, says Dr. Judy Garber, Director of the Center for Cancer Genetics and Prevention at the Dana Farber Cancer Institute, and professor of medicine at Harvard Medical School. Women who have gone through this diagnosis are at risk for getting it again. However, while about 25 percent of women are likely to have a recurrence in their lifetime, it's important to realize that this also means that 75 percent of them won't develop cancer again. Being honest with myself and you Diva, I pray over myself daily trusting God that I am healed and will never have to go through a reoccurrence. Even though I was strong enough to get through it the first time, it took so much out of me, and I don't see myself being as strong if I ever had to do it again. I love my annual doctor visits to see my beautiful female surgeon. Her hands are the ones that were guided by God removing the tumor with a perfect incision around my areola, and clearing the breast margins efficiently leaving no cancer behind. I feel forever indebted to her, and since she has seen me grow into my survivorship I would love to even invite her to attend my wedding one day! My male oncologist told me on a recent visit, *"I'm proud of you, and I'm sure you couldn't imagine your life the way it is now when this all first started."* My eyes filled with tears and gratitude hearing him say that. He treated my Mom and me with patience and care from the beginning, even when we saw him as the enemy quoting medical statistics and facts. Our faith has always been in God not man, but we had to realize God opened doors for me to receive the best medical care to get me healthy again, and my oncologist was a part of that process. I was even honored by my sister Krystina who used my story apart of a health class presentation for her nursing program in which she got an A on! Since then, I have been maintaining my healthy goal weight with my continued healthy lifestyle changes, which includes my new passion for hot yoga (*although I do sip a nice French martini from time to time nowadays*), and I have been continuously keeping up with all my appointments with my physician team through the years. As a survivor, it's surreal walking the same hospital hallways or sitting in the same reception areas when life wasn't so great. It just proves there is always sunshine after the rain. My life right now is so positive, full of so much love, growth, prosperity, and peace. I am doing everything in my control to stay healthy and do my part for my body which I am the keeper of. Most of all I would not want to put the two closest people to my heart, my Mother and the love of my life through emotional toil or stress. They need me in their lives for a very long time, as I need them in mine. I have so much to life for, life is so much more exciting now since I've grown and became this new woman. Since the Lord gave me a second chance of life, I gave him my heart again for a second time. I chose to get re-baptized at my church in front of a small group of my family and friends, so the *"old me"* could be washed away, and I would be officially *new* again through Christ. Healed and happy. It was spiritual promise to Jesus as my Lord and Savior, and a sincere thank you for His grace and mercy on my life. So Diva, appreciate having loved ones as a motivating factor to stay alive and become spiritual fulfilled so you can enjoy all the life possible with them here on this Earth. The love of God and your family is so important to keep you going, but you have to remember that the enemy doesn't have the final say; God has the final say. And He says, *"I will always cause you to triumph. Be strong and of good courage. The Lord your God is with you."* Joshua 1:9

In honor of a few prominent celebrity breast cancer survivors in Hollywood who won the battle against this disease, I am highlighting them for using their fame to raise awareness and inspire everyday women like us everywhere. Divas aren't made they're born!

Our Pink Ribbon Sisterhood includes:

- *Sex and the City star Cynthia Nixon*
- *Actress Christina Applegate*
- *Kylie Minogue*
- *Good Morning America host Robin Roberts*
- *Today show host Hoda Kotb*
- *Fashion designer Betsey Johnson*
- *Actress Maura Tierney*
- *Comedian Wanda Sykes*
- *The Sopranos star Edie Falco*
- *Olivia Newton John*
- *Singer Sheryl Crow*
- *Television personality and journalist Giuliana Rancic*
- *Chicago based Fashion designer Barbara Bates*

"The word Diva to me means doing something supernatural with something natural." – Patti Lupone

ABOUT THE AUTHOR

Deetria N. Cannon is a graduate from Southern Illinois University Carbondale with a B.A in Mass Communications and Media Arts, along with a Minor in Advertising. She has always enjoyed writing short stories and poems; English was her favorite subject through her adolescent years, advancing to Creative Writing courses while in College. She takes pride in *"Surviving in Stilettos"* as her first written book, inspired by her journey with breast cancer diagnosed at the young age of twenty-six. She stands tall as a proud survivor with God's grace and mercy. Deetria is a non-denominational Christian who carries a captivating smile and spirit, and a voice that is well respected by any audience. Her medical experience has inspired so many to increase their faith and believe in the impossible, while still looking, but more importantly feeling beautiful. She is a member of Alpha Kappa Alpha Sorority, Inc. and has a strong passion for the performing arts. Deetria loves her Shih Tzu Nino, and lives in the Chicago metropolitan area of Illinois.

www.ingramcontent.com/pod-product-compliance
Lightning Source LLC
Chambersburg PA
CBHW060844050426
42453CB00008B/815